THE DIVORCE AFTERLIFE

THE DIVORCE AFTERLIFE

The Lifeline Every Anxious Mother is Searching for During and After a Divorce

Jenn Logan

Jenn Logan & Co.

Beavercreek, Oregon

Published and printed in the USA
by
Jenn Logan & Co.
Beavercreek, Oregon

Copyright © 2021 by Jenn Logan

ISBN 978-1-7371978-0-5
FIRST EDITION

All rights reserved. No portion of this publication may be reproduced in any fashion, stored in a retrieval system, or transmitted in any way—without written permission of the copyright holder—except by a reviewer who may quote brief passages in a review.

Author's note
Names and details may have been changed to protect the privacy of those mentioned throughout this publication. Any views expressed or implied in this work are those of the author—this publication is not intended as a substitute for the advice of a healthcare professional.

Cover design by Author
Editor Marni MacRae @mmacrae on Fiverr

COB

All Love | in All Ways | Always

TABLE OF CONTENTS

INTRO 1

CHAPTER ONE – CIRCUMSTANCES 13
- BOUNDARIES 13
- CHATTER 25
- CRYING 28
- JUST BREATHE 30
- ACCEPTING 31
- SILENT KILLERS 40
- MARRIAGE PROBS 41
- WHAT MO WILL YOU CHOOSE? 48
- WELCOME TO YOUR DIVORCE AFTERLIFE 52
- YOU'RE THE MAIN CHARACTER 53

CHAPTER TWO – SOCIAL MEDIA 59

CHAPTER THREE – INFIDELITY 75

CHAPTER FOUR – FORGIVENESS 87

CHAPTER FIVE – DIVORCE DECREES AND CHILD CUSTODY ... 101

CHAPTER SIX – NICKEL TOOTHBRUSH 131

CHAPTER SEVEN – MONEY MATTERS 145

CHAPTER EIGHT – PARENTING ADVICE 161

CHAPTER NINE – HEALING 163
- EMOTIONAL WOUNDS OF DIVORCE 164
- SELF CHECK-INS 168
- VISUAL VACATION 169
- ONE THING AT A TIME 172
- WRITE FOR YOUR LIFE 173
- I JUST CALLED… TO SAY… 177
- YOGEE 178
- RELEASING AND LETTING GO 178
- IDENTITY 179
- FOCUS 184
- DON'T STOP BELIEVIN' 188
- HOW YOU HEAL 192

BONUS CHAPTER – LOVE AND RELATIONSHIPS 199

AUTHOR BIO 213

INTRO

A long-lasting marriage is what we expect when we say yes to someone who agrees to a commitment that big. I mean, that's what we all think going into a marriage, right? We believe with all our hearts that we're going to give it our best. And that *they* are going to give it *their* best. That we will commit to one another, under God, and that our commitment to marriage will only be broken by death. We believe that we are going to be the best wife and do what our husbands wish, and we will make them happy... and they will make us happy. We expect to have the most wondrous life together—to celebrate our 75th wedding anniversary while our grandkids look at us and think, *I hope to have a love like that one day; they make it look so easy.* That's what we think when we're standing at the altar, exchanging our "I do's," agreeing to a lot of heavy stuff that doesn't make actual sense to us at the time because we haven't lived through any of the "what if's" that our futures hold. We haven't encountered the better or the worse and the sickness and the health; we haven't been through the rich and the poor yet. And then... wouldn't you know it, life happens. People make choices. People get hurt. Then, people divorce.

I may be writing this to you from four years into my divorced afterlife future, but I was 100% in the same spot you are in now— holding someone else's book, praying to God to find a smidge of hope on how an anxious mother could survive a divorce. In my time of searching and seeking and desperately praying for hope and healing, I learned some things *for* you. I did some extensive soul work for *your* benefit. And... I intend to share things with you that I never thought I'd want to say in earshot of another human being. But I'm willing, because I believe it will help you; just like the honesty I frantically searched for and found helped me.

You and I didn't think we'd ever be in this kind of situation, did we? Surely not. No matter how old or young we are. Nope. No one does. That's a universal thought when we're divorced: *I didn't expect to be a divorcee.* Divorce breaks a woman down pretty quickly, despite our great adaptability and resilience that we've already learned from life itself. So, I can understand the cries of your heart right now in your hurting, as *that* is universal as well. We mothers have an unspoken connection that not all of us ever really acknowledge—at least not until we experience something like a divorce. But once we realize we are surrounded and supported by an entire community of women we may not have ever connected with before now, we begin to realize that we *will* make it through this, with the help of that silent connection.

I wrote this book because I am a living, breathing woman, mother, and human, just like you. And even though I've done months and months and months and months of soul work since my divorce, I still don't feel quite "good enough" sometimes. Totally a human move right there. See, I'm not afraid of honesty. I still have my shit days. And this is long after my divorce. How human of me, right? I still don't have *all* of my life together in the present day, either. Oh God, is my human showing again? No one really has their life all glued and stuck together, no matter how much you believe they do. No one. So even though I'm far from the time of my divorce, I'm still learning and relearning how to love myself fully and I'm still creating the life that I want every day. I'm not floating in my pool outside my mansion with a maid cleaning up after me while my children are learning 5 languages with their private tutor. Nope. I'm still making car payments and don't own a home. My children fight, and I yell sometimes. I'm human, and I'm not here to impress you. But I *am* here to completely acknowledge you and encourage you through your divorce woes—because I absolutely know I can.

I wrote this book with the intention to remind you of your value and importance. To remind you of all the remarkable things that make you who you are. To remind you that putting a voice to your own struggle with complete transparency allows for the deepest healing to take place. And to remind you that you're not done doing amazing things in this world; there's still so much of you that the world desperately needs!

My intent in these pages is for you to feel seen and understood in many ways. To feel my love and friendship. To feel more at ease about things. Just the act alone of you reading this right now is changing the chemistry in your mindspace and heartspace to a place of relaxation and calm—did you know that? That is so incredibly good for you right now. You're focused on something that requires you to be still, focus, and breathe steadily. Your heartspace and mindspace need a break, and you're making it happen in the most loving way. I never question your intelligence. Also... I'm not a robot. I'm a woman and mom— just like you. A person with first-hand recollection of the divorce experience. I didn't dedicate my precious and limited time on this earth writing these words with the hopes of becoming filthy rich. Nope. I choose to spend my time helping other women out. To help other mothers out. To help other humans out when they're knocked down in life and in spirit from a divorce. We *need* that for one another.

We *need* to keep putting help out into the world so it is readily available to those who are searching desperately for some sort of lifeline. Especially when it comes to divorce. I choose to use the good that remains in me after having to feel such devastation in my soul from this painful chapter of my life. You too will help other women out in the future when it comes to divorce, whether you believe it or not right now.

You may or may not cry through a lot of what's in this book. You may not even know what you're expecting to get from reading on from here because you haven't gotten much from it yet. You also might just skip over things you don't want to hear or are not ready to think about yet. Totally expected and absolutely okay. This book is yours—you can take your time, highlight passages, rip pages out, write notes in it, let your tears fall on the pages, use it as an umbrella… heck, you can throw this book in the trash can if you want to (but don't). All I'm saying is—there is a need in your heart for some reassurance that you're going to make it through this, and my promise is that you'll get it if you read this book in its entirety with the intention to fully receive its information.

When I was getting my divorce, just a month and a half after celebrating a 7-year anniversary, I didn't have a clue of just how much my life was going to change, shift, morph, and grow. How much I would grow. I wasn't prepared for any of it. You're not either, are you? Of course not. No one is ever truly "prepared" for a divorce, unless you've had one or two already. And it's highly unlikely you're reading this book if you're an ol' pro at the divorce game!

I was a child of divorced parents myself, but I knew so little of what was really ahead, from the adult side of things. I was now about to experience a bit of what my own mother may have experienced. And on the other side of that yucky, unavoidable truth was another yucky, unavoidable truth—my children were also going to experience what I experienced as a child. That one really hurt. Actually; both those unavoidable truths really hurt. There are unavoidable truths that are going to hurt now, and a little more ahead, but you're going to make it, and I will be right there with you.

I journaled quite a bit during and after my divorce, and many thoughts and feelings are included throughout the chapters of when I was actually struggling through some of the dark parts, in real time. If I go back now and read over some of those journal entries, I wince at the thought of some of those low places. So, I know exactly how low it might get for you, and that's why I want to talk about it. When I was where you are, I had young kids at the time— 3 and 6. Young, sweet kids that I never thought I'd have to explain what a divorce was with an actual, living example of the experience. I was in my thirties when I got divorced. Not quite grown up yet, if you will. Those ages may not line up with your timeline of ages, but that doesn't actually matter in this context. We're not comparing ages so our stories feel more relatable; we're acknowledging something more important here—what your soul, spirit, and psyche might experience as a woman and mother who is divorced, and how you might handle it best.

I didn't go through my divorce seeking revenge; I didn't have to build up walls lined with hatred to survive it. And neither do you. I have full consideration for you, and I'm going to be kind to you. I'm going to be open with you. I truly believe you need to hear both the beautiful and the brazen nature of some things you might be feeling and thinking right now—so you can feel seen over and over again. The <u>beginning</u>, the <u>during,</u> and the <u>aftermath</u> of divorces are filled with crazy thoughts and feelings. I'm acknowledging that part, from my personal viewpoint, no holds barred. They do need to be spoken of too, the crazy thoughts. That's part of the whole ugly process of divorce. And part of the ugly process of growth in life in general, right? The parts of every ugly process we go through in life, the parts that no one wants to hear or talk about, usually end up being where we get the most understanding and growth. It's the craziest thing how that works. You would think that people would naturally want to talk about all the yucky life processes we might go through if it helps other people. It definitely doesn't come naturally to every one of us to do so, though. It's intimidating to be vulnerable; imperfections showing for all to see, on purpose. Scary even.

I'm not at the beginning of my divorce anymore. I'm at that place so far away from the thought of my own divorce that when it comes to mind, it's likely an afterthought of sorts. But when I was in the thick of it all, it absolutely consumed and destroyed a large portion of me. It left such a specific mark on my heart; a mark that only another divorced woman would be able to identify, understand, and empathize with.

You'll feel love from me more and more as your mindspace rests on the words ahead. How I know this is because I'm writing from my experience. I'm speaking from a place of remembrance of what *I* needed to hear and how I needed to hear it. I also needed laughter! I remember how hard I had to search the internet just to find someone or something that said it was okay if I felt that my entire world was ending. I didn't need the other stuff. The other stuff that made me think I needed to be mad and hard and think hard thoughts and harden my heart up so it "wouldn't hurt." The stuff that would try and lead me down a path of big and drastic changes that would ultimately turn me into a different person altogether. There was plenty of that out there in the world if that's what I wanted to become after a divorce. But that's not what I wanted. I don't think that's what God wanted for me, either. And I don't want that for you. You do not have to harden up or toughen up to make it through this. You don't have to bury a version of you that you think can't survive this. The you that's reading this is already capable of remaining who you are at the core of your existence AND making it through just fine.

When the reality of a divorce is currently happening in our life, even *thinking* we will thrive in life again seems too heavy to hear. We are in our pain NOW, and to even think a happy thought seems wrong because this is not a happy time. I know it's hard to hear or even think that it will be better for you any time soon. I know it's hard for you to be in a different feeling environment or in different surroundings than you're used to right now. I know it's hard to think about money or the future right now. I know it's hard to be present with your kids right now. I know it's hard to hear or think about *anything* right now. I know, because I have been there. I have sat in your exact place, with the uncertainty of what the future held for me, for my kids, for our lives.

Every single thing is extremely heavy at the beginning. Heavy heart. Heavy thoughts. Heavy opinions. Heavy decisions. All heaviness, and getting heavier by the minute. Oh my goodness, friend, I absolutely know what you're carrying. I remember that weight. With that being said, and with all of my heart; I'm devoted to taking some of that heaviness from *your* mind, heart, and soul. I made a decision to express, explain, and expose my thoughts, feelings, and experience of divorce and beyond, so *you* can begin *your* healing with my reassurances that I do see your struggle, and I also see your way through it.

Some women will remain in the same yucky feelings and yucky thoughts that come with a divorce *long* after it's done and over—with no growth in any capacity. Some will even stay stuck with the yuckiness of it all forever. While others, *you*, will actually grow positively from it. Your perspective and experience are all you need to grow from here on out. The growth part *is* a choice though. A choice that only you can make. To me, when I speak of growth in the context of a divorced woman, I think of inner strength and love for self in order to weather the seasons of change ahead. I think of growth in this context as becoming resourceful, authentic, and humble in a very specific way. Growth becomes easier when you know and trust what foundation lies beneath, and since we know this is theoretically like ground zero, you know the initial strength it's going to take to lay that very first brick down—what it's going to take to lay them over and over again. I believe just you reading this right now is that first brick. Laid. You've already done it. You've already committed to your growth. I'm positive you've made your choice in faith.

What some of us women silently experience in our life after divorce can only ever be felt and never really explained properly. Oftentimes, when we are going through something hurtful that we've never experienced before, our own healing can only really begin when what we are feeling, thinking, and experiencing has already been experienced and expressed by someone else first. The reassurance we receive in hearing someone else's similar hurt often provides a bit of initial hope—in that you can make it through, too. I know some of us will only survive those really really tough days ahead by hearing or reading something that is *just* close enough to what we are experiencing at that moment so that we don't feel so hopeless and alone with our confusion and heartache. I will not leave you alone in any of the feelings and thoughts that you are likely to experience as you move onward and away from this part in your story of marriage. Your tender heart is all that I'm thinking of. This experience you're in feels heartbreaking, yes, but I assure you; your heart is intact and doing its job for you and is still filled with the purest love, I promise. You WILL survive this.

We sometimes survive our own divorce simply by knowing someone *else* survived theirs.

CHAPTER ONE – CIRCUMSTANCES

———⋅❦⋅———

The circumstances that lead up to the divorcing of two people really do set the tone for how you are going to survive and thrive in your life after your divorce—which I've come to refer to as: THE DIVORCE AFTERLIFE. What's ahead for you is the survival story of my own divorce, as seen through my own experience of it and told in the way that I believe will benefit you the most in your divorce survival story.

Here we go!

Boundaries

All of our varying circumstances within our former

respective marriages are going to be different. You have your entire story. I have mine. There are always two different sides of every marriage and divorce story; yours, and your former spouse's. And we'll only ever have the view from our *own* side to go by, right? Right. So, it is not now, and will never be, your job to learn about, grow from, and repair anything that may have been experienced from the other side. We can't learn and grow from the things on the other side of the story because we don't have that perspective, and we never will. We don't have that story. And you don't need that side of the story to get to where you're going, either.

Some of our stories and circumstances out there leave many women to start over, completely at ground zero. No money, no home, no one to trust, and no idea what to do. That's a big deal. Some of our stories have great losses and deep heartache in them. Some stories can make us feel used up and unimportant. That hurts my heart to write out because *I* felt that way. That's not what I want for us women; for you. That's not okay with me. But it happens daily. Many of us are also left with an overwhelming feeling of worthlessness—of being a nobody. This could be *your* deal right now. *Your* situation. *Your* story.

There are endless stories out there in the world, living within the hearts and minds of divorced people. The stories are kept safely closed forever in the hearts of some out there, too tender to ever open again. While some of those stories out there are filled with a wide array of experiences that are oddly similar to our own, others are so far out there that you can't even imagine the faith and endurance some people must have had to make it out okay or even have the willingness to share it with others. Some of those stories include daily physical abuse for decades. Some may have endured daily emotional abuse and manipulation. Some of us were cheated on. Some of us cheated. Some of us didn't have enough open and honest communication. Some of us didn't have any real communication at all. Some of those stories have addictions attached to them. Some of those stories have people in them who really didn't know the real person that they married at all. Some stories have people in them who stayed married just for the children. Some of us got pregnant and got married because of that but were never in love or loved. Some of us hated our marriage. Some of us were really young when we married. Some of us were a bit older. Some of us lost a spouse to death and it feels somewhat like a divorce. Some stories have years and years of anniversaries in there and some only have one. Whatever your personal circumstances were within your marriage that landed you here, holding this book—well, that story is important. *Your* story is important. That time is significant. It's a big deal, your story and your time, and it's very much the big contributor to who you are and how you feel today, right now, in this very moment as you read this.

Remember me talking about ground zero? Yeah, that low, low, low spot no one likes to start at after a divorce? The place where you know something was and should be but isn't? I was at ground zero. I was at that low, low, low spot. To me, my life was demolished after the divorce. All that I knew as a stay-at-home mother, and all that I counted on, was gone. Along with it was my self-esteem and identity. A few friends I cared about seemed to have gone with the demolition, too—right there at the beginning. Ouch. It hurt. All of it. You name it, it hurt. My sweet spirit and faith in all things good, and even God, was nearly gone at that time.

Everything changed so quickly within the first few weeks of knowing we were divorcing, and I didn't have much control over any of the rapid-fire changes. I felt like a spectator of my life versus someone who was involved, making choices, and being present in any given moment in those weeks. I was scared of the future, scared of my emotions, and scared of the unknowns of what it meant to actually get a divorce. Had it just been me, without children, I would have gotten through it a helluva lot sooner because the annoyance factor would have arrived real quick and I don't think I would have questioned the idea of moving away the next day.

But that was not the case. I was fully immersed in, and overwhelmed by, being a stay-at-home mother. I was knee deep in rearing responsibilities, stressed, depressed, and so far away from any sort of real genuine love for myself. And I was now also fully aware of my new responsibility with my kids and their soon-to-be-broken hearts. That was one real tough truth that was on repeat in my mind. The kids, and how divorce was going to change the entire stable landscape of their life as they knew it. That knowledge of what was to come for us; the big life shift that a divorce presents, was one of my biggest fears, aside from the death of a loved one. I didn't want my own children to experience sadness and discord in their hearts from something someone else chose for them. I thought they deserved better from me... from us. I didn't want to be a single parent. I didn't want to parent alone—God knows it's still hard even when you do have a bit of help! I didn't want to be sad and alone, either. But that's where it seemed I was headed. It hurt. It all hurt. You name it, it hurt.

Then, as if it was scheduled on a calendar; the outside chatter began to come in like a flood the moment my husband moved out. The chatter was scattered all across the land. The chatter *can* absolutely affect us in small ways *if* we listen. I was verbally encouraged several times to "just move on" with life, as if nothing had happened and no one had to discuss crappy behavior or take responsibility for anything. I roll my eyes at that term, "just move on," because it's *supposed* to sound strong and amazing and powerful to do as a human, but no one tells you HOW to do it, or better yet—how to do it *and* still have a heart and soul. It's so unnatural to get in that mindset as a human being with a beating heart.

The kind of person you are and the kind of person I know I am—we don't "just move on," do we? I was encouraged to move on by people who did not have my best interest in mind, mind you. Because that's what people say to you when they have no empathy, no experience with a divorce themselves, or they just really don't care about you. They tell you to just "get over it." Gah, that saying is so gross, too—*just get over it*—bleh. The heart and soul dies a little when that mindset is put into place. We're not doing it like that. We are made for so much more than to just get over things and move on in this lifetime.

It was hard to deal with, though—knowing that some people out there in our world expect mothers and their children to just move on through quickly. You know, like a rotating door—just keep it moving, sister. It was often radio silence when I asked for some answers and insight as to what was *really* going on with everyone. Answers I thought I deserved. Answers that I thought I might actually get if it would expedite my "moving on," as suggested. As I think about it now—I imagine that type of "encouragement" was coming from a place of personal pain, where closing off the heart was the easiest way to avoid processing some personal issues. Or maybe they were just jerks. Who's to say.

The beginning days and weeks of it all were all meshed together. It felt like a continuation of the same crappy day. I cannot recall sleeping or eating or bathing or going to the bathroom or blinking or even breathing during that time. Truly. It felt like two weeks of me being awake and doing things while crying and feeling invisible at the same time.

My stress and anxiety peaked every time I opened my eyes in the morning, when the rush of my reality flooded my mind and heart. When I awoke in the morning, I pictured my blood pressure level looking like a jagged red spike shooting straight up, like on a graph, and then tapering off again only after I laid my head down to sleep. Each day was completely intense and utterly overwhelming.

The love poured in from some of the closest people to me though too, of course. And of course, I still thanked friends and family when I received the well-intended comments about how everything was going to "be okay" … "in time" and my "kids are resilient." But I didn't believe any of it in those moments. I couldn't even register those words. I didn't want my kids to have to learn what resilience was through the divorcing of their parents. I didn't want things to be okay in time. I wanted things to be back like it was, before the word divorce was ever mentioned by either of us; even though that time wasn't super great, or even *happy*, really. That didn't matter though in comparison to how it was now. The *now* was absolute horse shit. I hated the *now* I was in. What I wanted most, right then in the early stage of it all, was for my children to have both their parents together in one home again, like it was. For *them*, not me.

Sometimes, parents may not be in an ideal marriage, but they'd rather stay in that situation than go through a divorce. You know why? Because *that* part is excruciatingly hard. The part with telling your kids. And all the parts that follow that hard part are hard too. That hard part doesn't feel okay to any loving parent. That part shouldn't be an option in our human experience, because divorce can break a child's good spirit down real quick. Right then, at the freshest stage of knowing we were getting a divorce, I wanted us to share meals and laughter and snuggles and tickles... as a family unit—completely and only for my children's sake. My heart was destroyed over and over again because I knew what was ahead for them. It was the opposite of a fun surprise party. I was holding on to big news that would instantly hurt them the moment they heard it, even if they didn't fully understand what it really meant. That part should not be an option in our human experience either... that part is like smashing the most beautiful pieces of art that you've ever created. Art that you absolutely love and adore. I didn't want to hurt my beautiful creations. I didn't want the separation to hurt *their* innocent hearts.

The separation I'm talking about was it being just me and the kids in our home now. Me, and the kids whose faces I was lying directly to about where their dad was, every day. My spouse had moved out before we even began divorce proceedings—the day after the kids started school that year. Awesome. Did I mention I was a stay-at-home mom? I'd been a stay-at-home mom for seven years. It just got better and better the first few days after he moved out, too! *Rolling my eyes so far back in my head.* As I looked at our bank account balance, it would appear I was now the proud owner of ninety-seven dollar bills, 3 quarters, 1 dime and 2 pennies. That's an exact number by the way.

Following that monetary treasure of a discovery—the volatile emotional roller coaster of my life had its RE-Grand Opening... and I won a season pass! WHEEEE! I now had a home I was living in that I knew I couldn't pay for, I had no clear idea of what was really happening with my husband outside of said home, I was lying to the kids every day, and people were lying to me or just withholding information from me that had to do with my marriage. There were so many rugs being pulled out from underneath my feet that I couldn't get up fast enough to prepare for the next one. What a mess. I felt like I was in a ridiculous 90s episode of the Jerry Springer show. You know, the one where more and more people keep coming out on stage to confess that they knew about all the plot twists and secrets of the dramatic situation at hand. And I was that guest who just sat there—eyes wide open, emoji style—just frozen with a stunned look, listening to the verbal vomit of what was happening to my own life in real time. It seemed as though everyone knew more than I did about what was happening in *my* life with *my* spouse and with *my* marriage. I literally experienced middle school all over again, as an adult, right there at the beginning. I had never felt numbed out like that as an adult. It was nauseating. Not being able to communicate openly and honestly with those I needed communication from the most was the most frustrating thing.

I had kids who still looked up at my face every day, not knowing what was happening behind the happy "scenes" I would provide for them. I tried to keep it as steady and familiar as I could, but I honestly can't remember even making food for them or tucking them into bed those first few weeks. And the recurring thought loop of having only $97 dollars and no plan of my own brought me lower and lower each hour. I hated what that number signified. I hated that I wasn't just thinking about myself and what my own plan was. I wasn't selfish like that, and I didn't really know *how* to think like that. The "me first" mentality was not what this stay-at-home-mom was used to.

I desperately wanted honest communication and some straight talk on how this was *actually* going to be okay for me and the kids. Not getting that communication was what actually catapulted me into making some firm decisions based on my own needs and on my children's needs. I got a bit selfish, thank God. It became a big turning point in me having to put up boundaries like a mofo. I was never good at that—setting boundaries. At that moment though, after the first weeks of separation, access to me was denied on all fronts. I slowly started to block people with my personal boundaries as well. It felt great—I never once felt bad! It was no longer about anyone else anymore. It was about me and my children. I had to cut out all the chatter, for me.

If you need to put boundaries up in order to listen to your own voice of reason without distraction right now,

DO IT. If you need to put up boundaries that only you know about and only you will keep, DO IT. Those are easy enough to do and super healthy for your overall well-being. Just a decision not to communicate with certain people at this time is a great personal boundary that will help with your stress level. You are not required to have a reason, nor should you feel a need to justify that action now, or ever. EVER.

My other revelation I had right there at the beginning weeks of heading toward divorce was the revelation with that good ol' bank balance. Remember how I said that I hated what it "signified" to me? Yeah, that number in our joint account signified more than just an amount of money at that point in my life. I wasn't mad about the actual money. It was far beyond the monetary value of it all. There's something you must know about me—I don't scratch surfaces with my thoughts, I dive deep in them. So, to me, that balance signified just how much power I allowed my spouse to have over me. And for a second, I let this yucky thought come over me—that the "value" that was left in that bank account was what he thought we were worth. And that really pissed me off.

Reality happened really fast after those first few weeks. My reality as a stay-at-home-mom became the reality that... well, that I couldn't stay at home and do that anymore. That thought was a panic attack waiting to happen, which I would actually experience in the near future for the first time ever. But right then, I was just pissed all the way off; at the meaning I put on that number, and at the end of the stay-at-home-mommy era. Because, when you are a stay-at-home-mom and headed into the divorced realm... life doesn't seem to have much meaning if you're not able to continue on as a stay-at-home-mother. We're all-in when it comes to parenting full time, and that job, as a mother, is the ultimate job. Because it's the only one we've got! The stay-at-home-mom gig is the ultimate sacrifice to most things that help keep our individuality intact. That's what I *was*. That's *who* I believed I was. That is where I felt ALL of my purpose rested. That is all I felt I had left of me—the stay-at-home-mother title. It hurt. It all hurt.

Is it somewhat clearer to you that you are absolutely not alone at this time in your life? I hope you already feel a little bit seen in your story just hearing a little about mine. I can picture you already. You're intelligent. Soft hearted. You're caring and beautiful in more ways than just your appearance. You're a bit tired, but it's from how much you love others and want them to be happy, loved, and taken care of. You're holding it together as best as you can, but you think you might break down at any moment. You didn't expect this experience in life, and you can't believe it's really happening to you. I also instinctively know parts of your struggle because some of our natural motivations and desires as women are, not surprisingly, universal. So, whether we know it or not, despite the differences in our circumstances that surround our separate divorces, we'll experience and ponder a lot of the same things when it comes to the divorce afterlife, on account of simply being a woman.

Chatter

OMG DID YOU HEAR? Did you hear that so-and-so are getting a divorce? I can't believe it; I wonder what happened. Did you hear about them splitting up? I knew it wouldn't last. It seemed like they were so happy. Did you hear what she did? Did you hear what he did? I bet it was because of their... blah blah blah.

Blah.

Blah.

Blah.

The newsflash of your decision to divorce will spread across the land, and all the villagers will discuss it, especially if you live in a township where everyone might just know who you are. Or not. Either way, it doesn't really matter who you are and where you live; the chatter *always* begins the moment one of you mentions your personal marriage business outside of just the two of you. It happens every single time. Expect it and accept this part of the road ahead to divorce-hood. It is an oddly normalized part of the whole sha-bang, and we all deal with it in some form. The chatter may be a small part in the grand scheme of things, but *all* the things that could affect us in small ways need to be noted.

Everyone *wants* to know or *thinks* they know what

happens *in* your marriage or happened *to* your marriage. It's because when they think they know all about it, they are happy theirs is "better" as compared to yours—yours being the marriage that appears to be crashing and burning. That's how people are sometimes, how humans are—it's all good as long as we're not the ones crashing and burning. Truth is, everyone has their own personal dysfunction and a ton of garbage that they don't like to talk about—divorce or not. That's why some people want to know what's in *your* trashcan when it tips over, so they can talk about that instead. Some people are truly interested in what your dirty laundry smells like. People do this so they can justify, rationalize, categorize, and scale it all against their *own* dysfunctional, but securely hidden, garbage. It's a funny little thing we do, isn't it? But—reminder, reminder, reminder—we're all human, and we *all* own huge dirty dumpsters that are full of shit. We *all* have dysfunctions, and our own dirty laundry has made us all flinch a time or two.

I say that to remind you specifically of our collective human-ness and the various, and sometimes messy, life experiences we may go through—like a divorce. This is one life experience not everyone will actually experience themselves—divorce. So be prepared knowing that some people that you know who have not gone through a divorce themselves might have something to say about yours! Therefore, at the very beginning of this emotionally-charged spectacle—that is your divorce—you have every personal right and all the personal permissions granted to ignore everybody and everything if you'd like. Not a joke at all. *At all*. Let everyone talk; let everyone hear what they hear; let everyone say what they say. It's part of the deal with a divorce, and frankly; it happens whether you know about it or not. You're not concerned with it.

Looking over what it was like for you, through *your* eyes, *your* side of things, not how it was presented or perceived by anyone else, your perspective only; that's what matters now. Your side of the story, even as you are still writing your story on this very day you are reading this. Your story is still going! You are a woman. You are a mom. You are the star of your story. And you are amazing. You're not *just* "another divorced mom." You're not *just* a statistic. You're not "just" anything! You are more than your best day and worst day and all the others. You are more than what your feelings and thoughts are saying you are right now. You are more than your divorce. Don't stay too long in any energy that tells you that you are JUST something. Even when it's your very own volatile energy. Lots of lies will pour in when you're in this vulnerable state. Lies that will sound an awful lot like it's being spoken to you in your very own voice. Remember what I'm saying about these little lies and try not to listen to every single little thing that enters your mind during this time. Just be aware that it *will* happen, and you know the course of action about giving yourself a break and being kind to yourself. You can call BS... even on yourself. Crazy weird, huh? That means forget everyone else and their chatter and opinions and input. And forget even yours when it's stuff you wouldn't dare say to your own child! CALL BS and replace it with something better... anything else! That means you hold on to the simplicity of just speaking to yourself kindly, giving yourself grace when you aren't speaking to yourself kindly, and trying again in the next moment and the moment after that. Keep trying. I see you.

Crying

Distraction works in some cases during healing, but the beginning allows for a full-blown snot dripping, ugly cry or two. Unavoidable. Be honest—can you go 10 minutes without wanting to sob? I couldn't. My soul hurt. It kind of happens naturally if you're emphatic and have a huge heart or, well, you are a mother. We're like that, aren't we? Mothers—we feel these life things that hurt in such a soul crushing way. We're so full of depth, yet the hurt seems to reach into every corner of our depth, and it doesn't miss a spot. Big hearts feel big things, you know. By the way; it's okay to weep often. You know that, right? Whether it's been two weeks or two months, don't you dare think, "I'm crying too much" or "I shouldn't be crying over this again" or "why can't I get it together?" No, no, no, no... you cry when you need to! It's natural, and it's self-made healing medicine and natural relief. You don't have to force yourself to feel strong or be strong or act strong at any time. You WILL get there. You will feel strong once again.

If you'd like to think about it a bit differently—crying things out is a strong choice. It actually builds up your emotional endurance when you allow yourself to feel the hurt at its deepest and most impactful time by allowing the physical manifestation of the hurt (tears) to do what it does. Take the pressure off yourself, and don't force anything upon yourself right now. That's a choice, and that's a start in self-care and self-love. Taking the pressure off yourself. Cry freely when your tears show up. Let that water flow through you, my dear. It's your body and mind and soul naturally relieving your person of the burdens in your heart. It's a cleansing cycle of the soul. Let it do what it does as often as it needs.

You're going to feel the most numb and at the same time; super charged up with emotion at the very beginning. I looked like an absolute zombie, going through the most basic of motions of parenthood; all the while trying to smile and keep things "normal" for my children. I know I looked half dead doing it, from my puffy eyelids from crying every day to my blank expression on my makeup-less face. It's okay if you've been feeling or looking like the walking dead lately, too. Just take one breath at a time and be in one moment at a time, even if that moment is filled with tears pouring down your gorgeous, zombie face.

It has been said that slow, deep breathing can change your blood pressure by regulating your heartbeat, thus changing your energy—did you know that? I didn't back then. I mean, I may have, but no one *told* me to do it when I probably needed someone to tell me to do it the most. So, here we are. This is the type of stuff you can expect more of from me, practicing small actions together. You might as well give it a go right now.

3 super slow, deep breaths . . . Go.

I know that slowing down and focusing on breathing deep doesn't seem like a priority at the moment when there are so many things to figure out and plan and organize and get settled and get under your control and... wait, wait, wait, wait just a second... Now, full stop. **Take another big, deep breath in and let it out slowly.** There's no need to skip ahead on the mental checklist we mothers have had since the day we gave birth to our first child. No need to let the mind go further than the very minute you are in. The future will show up on its own. Things will get organized. Things will get settled. Things will feel sturdy again. So, for now, just remember one breath at a time. That's it. That's all you need to do now. That's all you need to do when it gets heavy again. That's all you need to do when your mind is trying to figure out if that thing will work out okay on that Wednesday afternoon 3 months from now. One deep breath at a time to bring you back to the very second you are living in. That's all you need to do now. That's all you need to do tomorrow. That's all you need to do when someone tests your non-existent patience next week, and that's all you need to do when your lawyer bills start to arrive.

Just Breathe

This feeling, this place, this environment, these circumstances, this hurt, this chaos, this daily crying, this painful part will not last forever. I absolutely see your future and it does not feel like this. It will not feel like this forever. Say these things to yourself as often as you can. Write them down. I mean it!

- This will not last forever.
- I will not feel like this forever.
- I welcome and allow my crying to show up and cleanse me whenever it does.

You have been and you will continue to take just one single breath at a time through every single moment that you will experience in your lifetime.

My entire situation, circumstances, decisions, thoughts, actions, beliefs, and crybaby nature may not align with you, so listen for and hear what speaks to you the loudest—I know we'll align and connect deeply somehow. And most importantly, just know that I prayed over the one whose tear-filled eyes might pass over my words as their heart is hurting. I have so much love for you. I have so much understanding of where you're coming from. I hope you feel my love until the last page of this book. I see you. You and I are connected for life, and I am your biggest fan who is rooting for your soul to shine in this world brighter than it ever has.

Accepting

What I learned was that human healing starts *after* the acknowledgement and acceptance of whatever it is we are healing from, in that; your healing only begins when you acknowledge your marriage story and its ending on purpose—not when it bombards and overwhelms your mind and heart unexpectedly and at random. Your purposeful review of it, with the intention of accepting every part of it no matter what it is, and ridding it from yourself opens up space within you and allows you to choose what will take its place. In this case, hope in your new, wonderful life. Your divorce afterlife only truly begins when this part is done; not just when you get a notarized document confirming that your divorce is final. You will soon see why it is so damn important to start with acceptance.

Your marriage shows you exactly what you need to heal.

So, let's go! Let's talk about yours. Your marriage. "My marriage? I don't want to review that right now," I hear you saying. "I don't want to think about that right now," I hear you saying. I promise I'm not trying to inflict pain on your heart or stress you out. TRUST ME WITH THIS. We're starting at the beginning of *your* story. The beginning of the ending of your marriage. Don't let those abrasive words rub you the wrong way. You know I love you. But that is where you're at. Saying yes and accepting that your marriage is, in fact, *over* is exactly what your mind needs in order to grab onto a new mind-frame and new truths and new hope. What that acknowledgement and acceptance does is it tells your heart and mind that you are ready to enter into the next stage of thinking. Acceptance of big ugly truths fully gives way for different, higher, and healthier feelings and thoughts. It also allows yourself to feel confident about mapping out a new life direction for yourself.

When you're still holding on to the last known direction of life that included your spouse, you can't quite make out another route. You *want* to heal and move forward in a new direction that provides you with the views of life you want, right? Of course you do! In order to do so, you need to choke down your pills of reality, without a chaser. That means fully accepting that the marriage *is* over, and you will soon be divorced, if you're not already. That means you're not going to hold on to any idea that you will get back together, if that is something that you think might happen, or you want to happen. That means that after you've fully accepted that the marriage is done, you'll have to recount experiences that happened and be honest with yourself about how you responded then and how you feel about those experiences now. You'll have to accept all of that. Everything. You'll have to accept all the things that you didn't enjoy and cannot change.

That doesn't sound like fun, I know. It sounds like I hate you and want to make you cry more. I don't. It has a purpose for your good, I promise. Taking a look at what is "no longer" can be painful, especially with a divorce. It was painful for me to think about what *was* and what *wasn't* any longer. I know I cried a lot looking back over my married life; I had so much hard stuff to face and look over within my mind and heart, even though all I wanted to do was publicly announce the type of douche-baggery I felt I had just endured! BUT—the opportunity for your healing exists within your own behavior, not in the behavior of others. That's straight up fortune cookie truth right there. I realized the focus had to then just be on me and my own acceptance of it all so I could heal. The focus is going to just be on you now, so you can heal too.

The steady peace we women want and deserve, on this side of a marriage, only comes from introspection and belief. That's why the acknowledgement of your actual reality is key right now. You cannot heal from things that are outside of reality. Now, I know we're not here to chit chat about our marriages, especially when mine's over already and yours has just ended. But—and this is so important—you must know and remember what your own marriage was *really* like and how it *really* felt. Recalling some things about your marriage, now that you are not actually living IN it, will invite some of that direction in how you are going to move forward FROM it. If you are hoping to feel better and better each passing day, you've got to remember who the hell you are without the wife title, and what your core beliefs are without a spouse's influence. That's a big part of the new direction you're heading in.

Back to your marriage story. As the memories of the marriage are swirling around in your head and you're looking over how things feel at the moment, are you seeing some things more clearly now? Have you already had some big revelations about it because you were intentionally thinking about it? If not, okay. I understand that it might be too painful or maddening to think about it if it wasn't pleasant or if it's still pretty fresh. You *will* find value in these next steps if you can commit to this one thing of grabbing some paper and a pen right now—write some things out about what's in your mind and on your heart regarding how you're feeling today.

Oftentimes, it helps more than you think to see your thoughts and feelings on paper or on a computer screen and out of your head! It does nothing for you if thoughts are just swirling around in your head over and over again. They'll keep swirling around with no resolution, like a little eternal stress tornado. I don't want you to live in a state of anxiety like that. I know this because that's what I did to myself at first. It was a tornado in my head that kept picking up more and more crappy thoughts that I would give it, and it just swirled and swirled forever. Eventually, in the middle of the most heart wrenching and angry days, I began to make myself write it out. It was illegible, with grammatical errors all day, but it was no longer in my head—what a relief. It was intentional. If you're not the note writer/diary/journaling type, I see how this can seem like an exercise in futility, but I assure you; it can help you. If anything, just take a pen out and write *I hate this freakin' crap this woman is asking me to do right now.* Aaaahhh see? Fourteen words of expressed honesty is also a relief in some way. Okay, okay, at least you smirked a bit just then.

Seriously though, got your paper and pen? Ten minutes is all the time you need to think and write. It will provide you with clarity and maybe justification for your feelings, but most importantly, it will feel good to get it out of your brain—that's a win in itself. This action is one I want you to become familiar with—writing out thoughts and feelings.

Off you go. Reflect and write and take a moment to yourself. Then come back.

There is nothing I want you to do with anything you just wrote down. But when you do this next reflection and writing portion, I want you to look *back* in order to look *forward* with new hope. You may re-live a few things you don't want to. Or you may see things for what they really were and it will actually hurt for the very first time. We know that dwelling on the past is never a good thing, but this is traveling back in time with a purpose, remember. I promise this isn't a torture exercise. This part is <u>acknowledgement and acceptance</u> on purpose.

Pointing out a few big contenders and acknowledging these were factors of your marriage's ending is where some initial acceptance can take place. By doing this, some understanding and forgiveness and grace of the small stuff might even start to take root.

Now, listen, I am NOT asking that you accept and forgive some of these terrible behaviors that you may have had to endure within your marriage, but rather to have understanding that people who behave in such cruddy ways sometimes, have some really big problems within themselves. I'm definitely not asking you to excuse repeated shitty behavior, as I certainly don't. I do, however, know you understand that for some people, there are certain parts of their human condition that have consumed them, and it might not ever change—which is lifelong imprisonment in itself. What my point is, is that those big and bold behaviors, actions, and words that you may have experienced don't have to stick around in your heart and swirl around in your mind as if you have *any* responsibility in trying to make them make sense to you now. Any of the experiences that you are recalling right now are only for the purpose of inviting in your acknowledgement of it as already happening, nothing else. You're not looking back to explain *why* things happened, just acknowledging that they *did* happen.

If you are ready to forge on through some past memories in exchange for a bit of forward movement, let's go. Start out by using the prompts below to write out what you believe were some problems in your marriage that equated to the decision of divorce.

- Was there ongoing arguing?
- Physical abuse?
- Was there lying and deception?

- Were there alcohol, drug, gambling, or sex addictions?
- Was there known cheating?
- Was there money problems?
- Was there emotional or verbal abuse?
- Manipulation?
- Did your spouse loathe your snoring?
- Or did you simply begin to hate the way your spouse mouth-breathed on a Tuesday morning while scrolling through Facebook?
- Did you drift apart and it's not some huge deal but it still is really tough right now?

Seriously think about it and be honest with it completely. Not the mouth breathing and snoring—but the big stuff. After you've made your list, come back, and we'll go from there.

You have your list. You've looked it over, and you can confirm to yourself that you've acknowledged and accepted that all of those things on your list *did* happen within your marriage. Right? Good.

Okay, now answer the following prompts. If you can answer yes... write those statements out in "I" statements on the lines underneath... Example: <u>*I* accept that those things cannot be changed</u>

Are you willing to accept that those things cannot be changed?

_____

_____

Are you willing to accept that your divorce was the result of some of those things?

_____

_____

Are you willing to acknowledge and accept that you are not currently, and have no plan to go to marriage counseling together and that your marriage has completely ended in divorce?

_____

_____

And that's all for right now! Take a moment for yourself.

When you acknowledge your past experiences like you did, as something that *did* happen and that cannot be changed or altered, it reminds you of your power of intentional thinking, no matter how many times your sometimes painful past tries to run up to greet you in your present day asking for your emotional attention. You CAN do that, you know? Say the word to yourself. Your wish is your (own) command. Your intention is your (own) command.

You *Can* Heal What You Can Accept!

Silent Killers

As you will naturally glance back from time to time, unintentionally, I ask that you practice eliminating something from your thinking when you do. It's the feeling that often supersedes all other good feelings once it happens. It's the feeling of regret. Regret is a silent killer. It's no surprise that it's likely to come up in your thoughts when you're getting a divorce or shortly after it's final. You'll regret just about anything that comes to mind if it's something you haven't fully accepted. Regret often provides the illusion that we would feel better in the moment or life that we are in now, or we would be in a more ideal state of being with ourselves or in relation to others, if we had just made a different choice in our past. Regret is wishing for a do-over of decision making. Regret can haunt a 73-year-old grandmother with a choice she made back in her 40s! Regret is ruthless. It's awfully quiet about it, too; it's born in the mind and lives in the heart. That's why the "rewire" of acceptance *first* is what I want you to see value in. Acknowledging and fully accepting that all previous life experiences are final greatly minimizes the effects that our natural thoughts of regret will try to force us into feeling.

I was full of regret with how I *shoulda, woulda, coulda* spent my time, knowing that this is where I ended up. That's the one that starts the regret parade for so many women! Try not to go there; it's so important. Regret serves no one. You know this. It changes nothing. You know this. But it *can* stifle your progress and make you hate parts of the past, which means you haven't accepted it and you can't properly heal from it. You don't have time for that. Regret and guilt and shame all do the same thing—choke out the happiness and peace that is waiting on deck for you in the very moment you're living in.

It is your full presence and full love and full spirit that is needed on this earth right now. Don't allow all that good stuff you've got going on to die with the past or die from those silent killers. You're human, and therefore, I know it'll come up—regret, guilt, and shame. When it does, think of me yelling *intentional thoughts with the purpose of acceptance only* at you... followed up with a big hug of course. I'm right there with you as you're going through what you're going through. I'm not going anywhere.

Marriage Probs

Within every marriage are two sides of how it was experienced. You have just spent a little time remembering and re-learning what yours actually looked like, dysfunction and all. For my marriage, we obviously experienced our 7 years in very different ways, too. And while no two marriages are the same, there are similarities across the board for many of us. Just you knowing of some of our commonalities minimizes the enormity of your past marriage problems a little bit, doesn't it? We've all had them. You see, the ol' mechanics of marriages and marriage problems are not so incredibly unique, if you start asking around a bit. It doesn't make us lesser people when we discover for ourselves the exact dysfunctional mechanics of our marriage that led to our divorce—nope, it just showcases our human-ness rather prominently. That's absolutely acceptable and absolutely not something to give a damn about.

Any past moment or situation that has our personal guilt or shame written all over it only becomes regret if we keep looking back over it while forgetting our power in choosing acceptance, acknowledging our human-ness, and remembering our God-given value. Accepting each circumstance and situation and experience we've ever been a part of is a form of self-love. How is that self-love? Because we did our best with what we knew then, and we are doing our best with what we know now. It's giving ourselves grace. A break. That means when we're in the present—right now—today, we're doing our best with what we know, and that is all that matters. To do our best or to have done our best, or what we thought was best at the time, is all that matters. We're all first-time humans here, doing our best.

I'm pretty sure I was the first one who mentioned the ill-fated word divorce, years before it would actually be mentioned again by my spouse and then again by me—and then brought to life by the both of us. Later, I would realize that my good intuition was actually what prompted me to throw the word out there. The final time that I said it, at the ending part of my marriage, I said it out of grief; as I had just lost a friend a month prior and was still not okay emotionally. I said it out of frustration of feeling stuck in life. I said it out of the feeling of having no identity. I said it out of anxiety, exhaustion, depression. I said it out of a full-time-stay-at-home-mom tiredness. Yes, that is in a separate category all on its own. It is the kind of tired that trumps all other kinds of tired. You know the one. And, I said it out of my unwillingness to have some really hard conversations with the man that I married.

I didn't want to *try* to talk to the man who I hadn't had a real conversation with in a long time. I didn't want to *try* to explain how I was feeling and what I was thinking and what it was that I wanted and wished for in our marriage. And I didn't want to *try* to listen to him at all, either. I didn't want to face the fact that my unhappiness was a direct result of how little *I* communicated what I knew wasn't working for *me*. I didn't want to face how much we didn't desire the same things in life. I didn't want to admit to the monster-of-a-person I had become in certain aspects of our marriage, too. And I certainly didn't want to hear any robotic responses when I dared pour out my heart and soul into a conversation; a conversation I expected would leave me feeling emptied out instead of encouraged and heard. I didn't want to do all that because I was exhausted

43

at even the idea of trying to communicate. He might have been too, who knows. I only know what I know. Of course, all this was what *my* own perspective was like. *My* view. These are the things I thought and I experienced in my personal world. I happily admit to the fact that I was absolutely one half contributor to our marriage problems, and I absolutely know that my perspective was only a mirror of what I believed to be true. My perspectives of my marriage are mine. I own them all. And you are on your way to owning yours as well, because they are true to you and absolutely valid in every way.

Married people everywhere have some of those exact same perspectives—it's nothing out of the "norm"! Did I mention I was tired? I was tired of endless court dates and hearings and lawyers and discussions and paperwork about custody, already. Yes, those experiences were *already* part of my marriage, long before *my* actual marriage ended. I married into that experience as a stepmother. When we marry, we sometimes enter into a family dynamic that already exists, whether good or bad, happy or sad, dysfunctional or functional. It's not until we are fully immersed in it do we know how well that dynamic is working and what part we will play in that dynamic. New marriages have family dynamics that some are not used to. Some don't know how to navigate it all so well, having had no prior experience. This, too, causes friction to the moving mechanics of a new marriage; and serves as another example of a very common thing included in some marriages that has the potential to invite conflict and tension in.

I was doing my best with what I knew as a stay-at-home-mom, and I was trying my hardest to be a subservient, God-fearing wife... and trying to do it all with a cheerful heart. It didn't feel right, though, because I'm not sure I was meant to be a stay-at-home-mom for that long, but I kept doing what I was doing and didn't question if it was *really* working. And that is how you become exhausted and resentful and completely lose your own identity within a marriage. At least it was for me. That's how a woman can sometimes exist within a marriage, or cease to exist, really. That is how a lot of women out there are living in marriages right now as I type away. Completely without an identity other than as a wife and mother. Am I speaking to *you* a little bit? Are you hearing anything familiar?

Okay, okay, it wasn't ALL filled with just the yucky stuff, of course. It's not as if there was never love there, or fun and laughter and happiness and good times. There was. There was support and care, compromising, adventure, great talks, and shared interests. That lives and breathes within marriages everywhere. It's fascinating though that the amount of private struggles in some marriages versus what is presented to the world can be quite drastic in comparison. Again, such a human move to show we have our stuff together... ain't no thang.

There are some major issues within marriages that would make us fall over; knowing people live like that willingly. And then there are the little marriage things that most of us had to just learn to live with or agree to work on them together. But do we actually want to work on things these days? Rarely, right? It's more work! People don't want more work. We want LESS responsibility and LESS work. All of us! And that is why we sometimes end marriages like we do. We make little things the big things and downplay the big stuff. We forget commitments, communication, honesty, and faithfulness, and we reach for easier and replaceable. We really and truly don't know what anyone's marriage life is like outside of our own. A lot of marriages end up being really similar, though, if you take a closer look. Everything that had an impact on you in your marriage is part of what's to be mended.

A perspective to consider is this: **The choices we make are never the "wrong" ones.** There is no such thing as a "wrong" choice, really. Think about it. It is just a choice. And each choice offers an experience in a certain way. That's it. You made choices. You experienced things in certain ways. And you made it here. You're alive and here. Ready to make more choices; have more experiences in certain ways. Learn more. Grow more. Love yourself more. With no regret. Not even about that one time where you did that thing that you have imagined what you would have done differently a billion times since then. Stop! Don't do that, you beautiful woman, you. That is to be left in your marriage life story. Which is fully accepted as done.

You know your circumstances. You know your side of the story. You have skimmed over the entirety of your marriage now and accepted what it finally equated to. It wasn't easy. But you did it. Remember I told you earlier on that you would understand the importance of starting with accepting the truths of your marriage and divorce and where you're at with your current situation? It's one of the toughest things to do, accept truths, but it allows for the beginning of genuine healing. Avoiding truths could set you back so far later on down the road if you held on to some idea that it was different than it really was or that it was not really over when it really was or that something didn't happen when it really did. I don't want a false start for you. I don't want anything that's not serving you positively taking up your mindspace right now; as that could bite you harder later, causing emotional damage.

What you've read so far are *some* situations in marriages and some of the beginnings of the divorce afterlife. Some of what you've read you have already felt. Some of what you read might be just up ahead for you. What you've read are *some* of the circumstances, thoughts, and feelings that we women are left with. What you've read are familiar circumstances, thoughts, and feelings for many women who have been divorced. There are many dimensions to what a divorce actually puts us through, individually. And like with any life change, you won't see all the dimensions for what they are until you are way ahead of them.

See, when divorce is brought up, it is rarely just something we women brush off quickly while smiling, saying, "Yeah, I got a divorce" as if it wasn't a complete emotional and mental overhaul. When brought up, that statement sounds more like this, "I was divorced, and it was one of the most difficult times of my life." So how are <u>you</u> going to get through the difficulty?

What MO Will You Choose?

Want to hear the truth of *my* process at the beginning? Of course you do. You need to. You need to see how some women accept or don't accept things. You need to see more human behavior that will balance out what you're feeling right now. At times, I didn't choose what was best for me, mentally or spiritually, during my divorce—because I didn't *know* what was best for me and didn't *know* what I was doing. Duh. I'd never had a divorce before! I want you to learn from me in how you probably *don't* want to approach this. I can't wait for you to hear more about mine, because I actually believe with all my heart that you are leaps and bounds ahead of where *I* was at the time of my divorce, and I seriously couldn't be happier for you about that!

Here it is... and oh my goodness, some of it ain't pretty. Ready?

So, my approach was that I focused on all the bad stuff as a means to justify our decision of divorce. I wanted to convince myself into thinking I hated it so much in order to cancel out all of my scattered feelings as they were. I wanted to be mad so it would be "easier." You know that tactic, right? It is so freakin' easy to yell and tell someone off when you're mad. That is cake. And that is fine that I did that at the time... I did my best. I see now that it wasn't actually helpful to me and I was moving so very far away from self-love and healing. Looking back over my marriage, I focused on every sideways comment, gesture, or situation that I felt was directed at me because I somehow "deserved it." And that perspective got me angry. That was survival mode for me—hyper focusing on everything that was in the past that was upsetting or undeserved or outright cruel—without any thought of accepting any of it as already over and done or putting it to rest in my heart and mind.

At the time, I was thinking solely of what a selfish liar my spouse was and nothing else. I wasn't looking at it to learn anything. Or to try and let it all go from my heartspace. Or to see something more clearly for my own benefit. I wasn't looking at *my* hand in it, either. I wasn't looking to accept the things that already happened. I'm not sure any of us would just naturally do that right at the beginning anyway. That is so hard to do! But you know the overall purpose of it now, right?

See, what I did was; I focused on every single crappy thing I could think of that had to do with my ex within the marriage story. Yup. That's what I did. I summed up the marriage that was over with—with all the shitty parts— and wrapped it up nice and pretty and threw the thought of the whole entire thing in the trash. That's a survival mode move right there, one hundred thousand percent. You feel me? I know you do. You may be sitting there relating to *that* mode of operation more than any other mode you've read about so far. Cool cool cool cool—it's certainly an instinctual mode; to not look at *why* we are so quick to throw stuff in the trash that once had meaning. That's heart and soul protection. That's self-preservation at its finest. That's innate. We instinctively know we don't like that kind of pain, and that instinctual mode sure helped get *me* through some of the tough parts at the beginning, I know that much. It was either I think angrily like that a few times or cry and be sad with myself and have a complete breakdown—which I would actually go on to do in the future (it's in another chapter).

So, I changed it up and got good and mad about it all, and I blamed every last thing on him. I didn't hold on to any such idea of us getting back together because I didn't want that at all. But I also didn't acknowledge the things in the marriage properly and didn't intentionally accept the finality of it enough to begin actually healing myself. You're WAY ahead already, because you see a few options you have... you get to make a choice, instead of doing what I did— heading straight to hate. Okay, it wasn't really full-on hate; I don't think that's in me, but you know what I mean. I was mad. Full-on mad.

It's okay to be wherever you're at with all this, by the way. I know which mode is better for you, and so do you.

It's not the latter. It's not full-on mad mode. It's not what I chose. BUT it's okay if you're there. Truly. I see you. I was you. Just breathe.

Your process through all this is not a straight line with check marks. There are no mile markers to show your movement through it. There are 50 different ways you could choose to approach your divorce afterlife, and there are 50 different mindsets that you could adopt along the way—both positive and negative. I experienced both ways in how I was trying to deal with the process of divorce and right afterward. I see both modes clearly now, and I know exactly why I chose what I chose when I chose it. I did *not* see the importance of accepting a few difficult truths up front. That's a tough thing to do when you've traveled through a lot of dark times in your life. Accepting truths that hurt you directly at the hand of other people or what you *believe* were at the hand of other people—that's a tough concept to fully grab onto in life in general. But that was key.

In not realizing that instant benefit of acceptance of every single thing I could never change or get the repentance that I thought I deserved from what hurt me, well, it kept me at a standstill in my process for a bit. Like I said, there's no guide as to how it goes here for you, no boxes for you to tick. It *can* be like that if you want it to be, of course—with check marks by all the movement and forward progress you're making. Or all over the place but still moving in the direction of full confidence and complete healing. You can choose to start with whatever you need to survive, but the needle *will* shift to whatever actually makes you feel better inside as time passes. You'll know it when it happens. You'll know what mode you're in when you start to feel better and think better; it will feel effortless, and healing will work in double time for you when you're there.

Welcome to Your Divorce Afterlife

So, this is it. Here you are. You have arrived, yet you are ready to keep moving forward. You are hereby reminded of and know *exactly* how to look over things when it's needed. Intention, purpose, and remembering your value remains the same no matter what you've accepted in your story. You have accepted a few hard things. And in doing so, you have created forward movement for yourself. You have taken complete ownership over all that you are doing from here on out. You are now operating alone. You're the pilot. You are now a solo parent. And whether or not your soon to be ex-husband is still in your household, on the next block with someone else, in the next city, in another state, or on a different continent, you've accepted it. It literally IS WHAT IT IS. Your reality.

YOU are now the only one in control of your own life, entirely, simply, completely, and thankfully. That's it. This is a newfound perspective, I know. Never seen life from this vantage point, have you? I know! I know it's not magically going to feel better just because you thought about a few things with that informal writing assignment I begged you to do, and I don't expect your excitement to peak realizing that you're the only star of the show that is your life now, either. These are higher frequency ideas of how to think of yourself and for yourself and how to place even higher value on yourself. These ideas and thoughts I'm suggesting offer you more ways to reclaim your own power just by entertaining them. They're meant to spike your confidence level over and over again. You might not enjoy being the center of attention while starring in your own life movie, but this is reality—you're the star! And you are absolutely brilliant at it, by the way. You're a smash hit, babe. You've already received a nomination for an award. And spoiler—you win.

You're the Main Character

Do you know what being you-centric is about and what it means? It means that you don't need commentary, input, or energy from anyone outside of yourself. You're taking a stance, and you're going to show up for yourself like you never have before. You're going to give yourself grace over and over again as you choose the things that make YOU happy over and over again. You are capable of making faith-filled, deliberate decisions that correspond to your intuition on what, where, who, why, and when—no matter what future decisions *any* of those words apply to. Any decision you make now is the one you feel good making. Just make them. Anything that needs to be taken care of, you can take care of. Say it to yourself out loud or write it down in the best penmanship you can commit to right now:

I am taking care of what needs to be taken care of.
My decisions are my choice, I trust my choices and I feel good while making them.

Those statements also apply to communication with your ex-spouse as well, if they are going to be around. Please know that unless you have an amazing and honestly supportive relationship with your ex already, and your ex isn't already with someone else, you do not need the very biased opinions or input of someone who doesn't care about you unconditionally enough to still be married to you! You just don't. At all. I promise that is all said out of love. It's not choosing bitterness or full mad mode; it's holding yourself in your own highest regard because you matter more than anyone else in this world. (Stop that. Stop thinking "What about my kids and my family; they matter to me too. Isn't that a mean thing to do—not consider them?") STOP. We all know we love and adore the people we love and adore, and we would likely choose death than any harm coming to any of them, EVER... but refocus! We are here for **you** right now. JUST YOU.

As far as you are concerned, the world is going to rotate around just you right now! Weird, huh? Take that fun little concept and flow with it. That's how much I want you to embrace the you that you are at this very second. The whole woman that you are, with every single scattered thought and feeling that lives in you right now. With the world revolving around just you right now, it also doesn't matter what kind of visitation arrangement your kids have with their dad either, and the frequency in which you will actually see one another. That doesn't change how *you*-focused you are going to remain. It is all about YOU.

You know how to remain genuinely kind and respectful. That's a part of who you are as a grown woman and amazing human. Remember, you don't have to people please right now. Or ever, to be more specific. **You do not ever have to people please**. There, that's better. You don't have to orchestrate or control any part of life that is outside of yourself to make others feel more comfortable with *their* life and in *their* moments with you, either. You don't have to caretake any part of any situation with your ex. You are not to be concerned with anyone but yourself at the moment and how you are feeling. If you are a believer, this of course does not mean forgetting about the relationship you have with God. Obviously, keep that going strong.

But I want you to love yourself so much right now, like you never ever have before, and to do that, you have to pay attention to just yourself, because you are it.

YOU will be the one who stays consistent and comforting for your children. YOU will be there for your children to answer the hard-I-don't-want-to-answer-these-questions, questions that will inevitably come up as time moves on. YOU will give the explanations of life's happenings (the separation and divorce). YOU will lie to their faces in order to protect their hearts from the devastation of their new, divided life. YOU will witness their changing demeanor because of their unspoken intuition that something is *already* different. And YOU will hear their responses and see a little bit of innocence leave them because of it. YOU will have the follow-up talks to make sure they are doing alright during this life transition. YOU will see your daughter get dressed up and make sure everything looks perfect as she waits by the front window, looking out at the end of the long driveway thinking her dad is going to be driving up to see her any minute—all while knowing he's a state away and has not made any plan to come visit her. And YOU will be the one who dies inside a little bit every time you see the longing in your children's eyes as they notice other fathers laughing and playing with their children at the park or they stop and observe a family that resembles what they used to have before the change.

It is YOU who will continue to be there for them as if nothing has changed. And *that* will be one of the hardest things you have ever done. You need to take the time to make it all about yourself and do what you need to put a smile on your face so you can continue putting one foot in front of the other as you walk this new life path! You need every single ounce of self-love you can muster up every single day because this experience will take a toll on the most resilient heart ever created—that of the woman and mother. It is about YOU and *how* you are going to take good care of your own self so you can take good care of your kids. You have every right to think about yourself and put yourself first. That goes for anything right now. I know, I know... you've never thought like that, have you? Well, at least not after you had kids or a husband. I know, I know... you always massaged the situations like a mother does, with the Mother/Caretaker instinct that comes natural to most of us. I know it feels like you'd be hardening your sweet, soft heart if you approach it this way. But that is just the opposite of what you are doing by putting yourself and your own thoughts first, especially now.

What you are actually doing is you are loving your children in a new way by choosing what's best for you (the mother) first. Weird thought, I know. Even if it means feeling like you're not being "yourself" when you put yourself first. I felt like I wasn't being "nice" or a "good" person when I chose to put my own happiness and well-being in a top priority spot. Isn't that complete nonsense? Read that sentence again. Nonsense. And that's an automatic thing for a lot of us moms. Holy crap. What a weird sort of relief when you realize you don't have to think about making someone else's comfortability a priority! Revelation of revelations right there.

Choose YOU. I insist.

Having the role as Mother and being in the position you're in right now is forging something within you that will empower you in your future in a very specific way that you would never have gotten any other way in this life—guaranteed. Keeping things focused on you, as simple as possible, is all I am asking you to commit to wholeheartedly. Commit to yourself. Commit to making life comfortable for you. No one is evaluating you or your performance as a mother or daughter or friend or anything else right now. No one is waiting on a reaction or command from you. The level of self-care and self-love I want you to reach is massive. If you're already doing that—freaking amazing, keep it going and recommit to loving yourself every morning. If not, start today. Keep it simple. A simple, "I LOVE YOU, self" is a start.

No one expects you to move on with it quickly. And anyone who asks or expects you to do this does not have a single second of experience with it. Humans are emotion filled beings, and you need time to process your experiences through your own filters or through the filters of those who are helping support you in healthy ways, and you certainly need to do this in your own timing.

CHAPTER TWO – SOCIAL MEDIA

———⋄———

I could write an entire book on my thoughts on the negative effects of social media and our psyche (and I just might). So, of course, I must touch down on it with respect to your current situation. So, I was logged into Facebook for only approximately 4 hours in 4 years. You heard me. Read it again if you think you just read the biggest typo of the century. I promise you, that sentence has been triple checked for accuracy.

I'll tell you about it in a few moments. But first, have you ever read a horoscope and really believed whatever it said was true and you were expecting it to come into play in real life? Or have you ever read a horoscope and manipulated situations and actions throughout your day to somehow make it line up to what it said? I have. I've also listened to tarot readings and literally shaped my mind and attitude around the life story the shuffled cards displayed! Silly, right? "Self-fulfilled prophecy," some call it. "Manifestation," others. There are also the meditations and affirmations that help us relax and also assist in shaping our healthy self-talk and help create belief that we can make the life we desire happen. You heard of all these things, yeah? You get where I'm going here, right? I know you are an intelligent woman. I know you understand the correlation between all of the things I just mentioned above, and social media; that plays a big part in our emotional health and well-being. The things we see and hear—even if untrue or skewed—well, we can end up believing a lot of it to be true at the face value it's presented at. Which it is—ALL face value.

It is really hard not to take it all in as reality these days, with all the screen time we are logging, in the good ol' 20th century. I know you understand the effects social media has on each and every one of us. So, I know you are not surprised that I'm putting this in here as a reminder to choose what serves you best and what preserves your well-deserved, often hard to come by these days, good, positive energy. I'm reminding you that you are curating a daily practice of caring for and loving yourself. You are the center of the universe and the world is rotating around YOU, remember?

Social media may be the number one thing that keeps you stagnant in you moving through the first stages of your divorce afterlife in a healthy way. I do not want to see you get stuck, not even for a day, in your self-love progression. I don't want you to have more shitty days than what's already inevitably forecasted as you go through this. So, social media is a big no-no right now. You hear me?! I bet you're thinking "I know this lady writing this book isn't really asking me to get off social media right now, is she? Who does she think she is...?" Well, I'm the one who sees your amazing future ahead of you, and I am absolutely asking you to *willingly* do that very thing—give up social media.

Think you can swing it—no social media? Give it a shot, yeah?

Let me tell you the big WHY behind my plea to you.

Would you agree that your life is no one's business but your own? Would you agree that some people can really get under your skin or make your skin crawl with their words and behavior? Would you agree that the talk of religion and politics can divide friends and even families? Would you agree that opinions and facts are sometimes hard to separate? Would you agree that your forward progress through this hard time in life has everything to do with mental health, physical health, support, love, faith, and hope? Would you agree that other peoples' lives are none of your business either? I'd be willing to bet you agreed with all of those things. Of course you did; you're smart. You're handling your own business, and your business is your own business on how you are going to move forward from this divorce. If you really do want to bask in the whole-est and greatest version of you, you have got to stay away from the toxicity that social media instantly brings to your table, every time. You name which social media platform you're thinking of when I say social media, and my response is— yep, that's the very one that can destroy your inner peace and throw you out of the self-love club with a quickness.

If you find comfort and encouragement in the words of others when you share your every single crappy post-divorce day, that is great if it is TRULY comforting and encouraging. But it will get old. The personal life diary megaphone that social media is gets annoying—even to ourselves at times. The encouragement you feel will become briefer each time. The comfort will be shorter lived. And in that time where you are receiving what you think you need from it, you will have not done anything within yourself for yourself. You will be exchanging your precious time looking for hope in others instead of creating it privately and for long-term by yourself. There is a healthy balance with all of this social media stuff, yes, but for now, your time and attention are all on you, remember? That online "comfort" is temporary. ALL OF IT. And you're not guaranteed a "good time" or a "good experience" every time you log on, either. That's a complete game of risk with your emotional vulnerability as it is. Social media is a volatile, unreliable source for what you need the most right now, which are the things that are fine-tuned to you, that uplift your spirit and feed your mind with ideas of a calm and happy life. Get rid of *anything* that doesn't work with that idea.

You're getting your new footing. You're pouring and setting your foundation, outside of any influence that doesn't come directly from your own needs and desires. You're keeping your days simple, and you're deliberate with where you put your time and energy. See, when we log on to social media platforms when we're in a state of vulnerability of some sort, we want connection. So, we say we are feeling some sort of way, fully expecting and knowing our post or engagement will get the attention we are seeking, for a moment. We feel seen. We feel heard. We feel validated in our current feelings and emotional fragility. It *does* work! Of course it does. I've done it. You've done it. We have implemented social media into our existence in a very creative manner, into the human race. We've conditioned ourselves to rely on its instant connectivity for praise through life's victories and acknowledgement of our misfortunes, unfortunately. I have experienced this time and time again with social media, and you have too. And that all feels well and good at first, yes. Until it doesn't anymore.

When you log off and "disconnect" from everyone, and you are back in your real reality and your real feelings, thoughts, sadness, and possibly hopelessness—*that's where the truest and long lasting self-encouragement* shows up… or doesn't, if you don't have a bit of that established already. The encouragement that you can only pull from your own self or from God or higher self cannot be continually broken up by the input and output of others. The cyclical mental and emotional energy surge and depletion when you're on social media is absolutely soul draining, and it can start your initial healing cycle over and over again. I know this to be true. You know this to be true. I have relied on social media to front me some encouragement or a "good mood" for a bit, but damn, that crash is hard afterward at times! And sometimes the encouragement doesn't even come! Social media is like drugs. And we all know drugs can kill good, vulnerable souls; and fast.

In the beginning of this new life, there is so much healing on so many levels that are very personal to each of us. We cannot willingly just let anyone have a say in how we are "supposed" to feel or how we "should" be so pissed or devastated or angry or upset. When we ingest the personal diary megaphone moments of everyone else's lives on all the socials, guess what feelings and thoughts we are going to immediately adopt and experience? You got it—everyone else's. That's overwhelming. You're going for simple and quiet right now, remember? That's the self-fulfilling prophecy horoscope type stuff I'm talking about. You'll do this almost automatically. Even if you logged on in a neutral mood, you'll log off completely divided from your own thoughts and beliefs and hope. It'll take you a good while to recalibrate back to your very own.

WHAT GOOD DOES THAT DO FOR YOU?

No good, that's what; you beautiful woman, you.

Is it just being seen that makes you feel better? I get that. So much so; I needed that at the beginning. Bigtime. I remember telling one of my best friends that I feared the kids and I were going to move away and no one would even remember we existed after this divorce. I said that because I knew I wasn't going to log on to any social media and say anything about what I was going through. I knew I wasn't going to say shit online about any of it. And... I didn't. I know being seen at a time like this is both wanted yet hated. Wanted for the acknowledgement of existence alone but hated for being seen at a crappy time in life like this. I understand. Divorce aside, we'll accept encouragement anywhere we can get it these days because living on planet earth right now is tricky. But what will be the most empowering and encouraging for you is not risking your own personal thoughts and energy for anything or anyone. There's always a mental health risk with social media. The risk is 50/50 on how you might feel after you've spent time online; it's either positive or negative. And I'd venture to say the majority of people would agree it has increasingly become more <u>negative</u>. Social media will always be there for you later, but for now, you are your priority. You are worth protecting your good-good energy for.

Does it sound extreme to you, hard even, to stay away? I know it does. We are all so used to it. You can do this though. You are here to pull that strength that lives in your depths, and not log on to social media for a while starting right now. Nope, don't even say anything about it... just do not log on. Better yet; just deactivate. It'll still be there, no worries. I'm here to help, so I'll give you an idea of what you're giving up so you don't go into panic mode just thinking about the idea of not logging in to "connect" with others.

First, you will avoid the feeling of shame. Shame? Yep, shame of your marriage not working out and you and your spouse splitting your kids' household up. Don't think you'll feel that by just logging on and scrolling for a minute? Don't think you'll feel shame? You will, if not straight up consciously, you will subconsciously. You would register that sense of shame when you see ANY other married couple post shit about anniversaries or surprise dates or memes about husbands not picking up laundry or seeing kids doing anything with both parents together.

Shame, shame, shame, shame, shame.

You will feel that at your core, and it'll hurt long after you log off. Even those beautiful family portraits that bless the social feeds will make you feel a sense of shame for not "holding your marriage together" in *any* way you could, while others, seemingly flawlessly, can. And the tricky thing about it all is: you won't even know you are being affected by it. But you will be. It just takes place internally as you consume social media. Sounds delightful, doesn't it?

Next up, you'll have the knowledge of who *is* and who *is not* behaving like a "friend" to you at a time like this. Ouch. That's a big one. This silly little realization/assumption of sorts happens on social media even sans a divorce. Isn't that funny? No. That shit is not funny. That shit hurts. Yes, it's okay for us to say it still hurts us as full grown adults. Again, you won't even know it's happening. You'll start to notice who is not "supporting" you. And that'll make you wonder if these friends of yours were always just silent a-holes or just suddenly became them now— when your marriage has ended and you could use a virtual hug, or just get any acknowledgment that you exist to them... at all. This knowledge will make you mad. Unknowingly though, remember, but the effects will go straight to your brain and heart. Excellent!

You'll also start to get sad seeing the people whose lives just carry on while your life just changed so dramatically; when your life and your purpose feels like it's on pause. Seriously, seeing life just press on when your heart is hurting... well, it just plain hurts; it really does. When you log on, you'll notice the world not revolving around your sorrow, and it won't feel good at all. Actually, when you log on to social media in *any* emotional or financial state other than happy and loaded, you are going to magnify every single thing that is not perfect in your own little world. Comparison is a killer and it's literally 100% unavoidable when you log in to any platform where there are other humans involved. I promise you, there aren't enough funny memes, fancy-fonted hot pink bible verses, or enough likes out there to make you feel like everything will be okay. "Logging off" never equates to the instantaneous unplugging of your heartspace and mindspace from whatever you just read or heard or saw or engaged in. Oh no, no, no, it doesn't work like that. At times, I am still upset or rattled to the core to the point of tears, or wanting to fight, at some of the things and people I have engaged with on social media—even hours later! That is some heavyweight impact it has. You know this to be true if you think about it. Is that a place where it sounds like healing a hurt heart and finding a steady stream of hope will be found? Not at all. That will be one of the most triggering and soul consuming places you could enter in the beginnings of your divorce afterlife.

Our own personal perception of our current life experience we are in is the most important. We can miss the opportunities to learn more about ourselves and appreciate ourselves further with every distraction and comparison that the socials offer. We cannot be led or directed by other humans who have their own problematic human conditions they are dealing with. Your own life compass is your only trusty guide to get you what you need. Which brings me to the last part of my plea for your great social media purge:

Do you *really* want to know? And for what?

Did I *really* want to know what my soon to be ex-husband was doing after he moved out and after we moved away? Yes. Duh. Of course! I wanted answers to all the questions I had about what the hell he was thinking and what was more important than me and our children! I wanted to know that stuff! I also wanted to confirm everything I already knew to be true about him now. We all want answers and reasons and explanations to things in order to justify our reactions and responses and recourse. But, for what? To keep moving in life, of course! Or at least we *think* that's what we need it for.

See, I thought it would make me feel more validated in my hurting if I proved to myself he was exactly what I thought he was at that moment. So I *did* lurk in the beginning... and it revealed all of the things I *thought* I wanted to know. Turns out, I didn't want to know all of that; it made me hurt more. It made me hurt more because to me, he was now one of those people whose life just went on without a pause... without us. Ouch. *The show must go on* is what I always thought of my time of lurking. Yuck. Oh but no—how unattractive—people don't *want* to admit that they browse around other people's lives while growing with rage, envy, bitterness, and resentment over the calm waters others are sailing in their yachts on when we are in the middle of the ocean on a patched-up innertube. Guess what? I know many people who peek around and go digging and searching, like the little social media PI's that they are. And right now, I'm certainly not afraid of this admission of being one of them at times, as long as I get this point across to you. Which is: You will *always* find something to make you feel like shit if you are looking for it. Always. Same goes for positivity, gratitude, inspiration, and love. You'll find what you are looking for. It will show up for you or you will make it happen if you're focused on it. This can be used for good or not. You know this to be true.

Did I *really* need to know about other people's lives in detail when mine was becoming unraveled? No. We talked about this earlier. None of my business. It crushed me even more. And it will you, too. Do not do that to yourself. I forbid you! Okay, I can't actually *do* that... but I wish I could if you don't fully accept and see the likelihood of social media being a detriment to you versus the slight possibility of it being a benefit to you.

When I logged on, I took an emotional hit every single time. I knew better... **But,** as it turned out, I re-learned that all *for* you—you see? You do not have to go searching for the answers you don't really want. You will never get ANY answer during or right after a divorce that will be satisfying to you—no matter what it is. Answers don't repair damage. Answers don't mend hearts. Answers don't rewind time. That is never what answers to our prying questions are there for, anyhow. They aren't there for our validation of feelings. They aren't there for repairs. So, don't go searching for answers unless you're ready to do the inner work on yourself. That is really the only way getting answers can change a situation—in that we ourselves will learn and grow and change in ways that honor our higher self and deepen our love for self when we have more information on what and why things hurt us like they do.

Take the social media apps off your phone. Or better yet—deactivate. Take away the temptation completely. Commit to it for a good while. Commit to <u>you</u> and breathe easy about your decision. You still have a phone; use it like a telephone and not a computer and connect with your support system that way. You can get the same encouraging words with the use of actual voiced words from friends who would love nothing more than to talk with you, love on you, and get you all gassed up about how amazing you are. Let them know that you aren't going on social media for your own sanity. They'll get it. And they'll love you and support you just the same.

How could I possibly know all of these different scenarios to be true if I only spent 4 hours on Facebook in 4 years? Because I'm smart. Because of first-hand experience. Socials have become a tool that feeds us hate via division and lack, but makes it look pretty. It is only when you step back, then step back more, then step back more, to the point where no one else has the vantage point that you are viewing from, that's when you see things for what they are and how the patterns of people appear. You know this. Had I kept logging in every day, my already really long healing time would have been quadrupled because I would have subscribed to the thoughts and opinions of others in my time of emotional instability. It is, of course, no fault of anyone trying to help encourage or justify your hurt feelings, as people who care often do. No, that is all sweet and well-intended and a thoughtful, welcomed gesture. But the psychology of how that all works for us isn't always positively beneficial. That is the main purpose of breaking down all the social media stuff and taking into consideration the true affects others have on us in our lowest and fragile moments.

You must curate the healthiest environment for yourself. You know what that looks like to you. You know yourself.

My plea for the purge still remains, however; there are a few positives too with all the platforms to connect to—just not as leveled as the negatives. What you can expect is people wanting to show their kindness and support, and that is the greatest feeling, no matter what the circumstance is, truly. Expect people to reach out to you when they hear of your divorce. People who you may not generally even really communicate or engage with in real life. It will happen. They'll say whatever they want and support you however they want; that is feel good comfort in its own way. Read their private messages and listen to their voicemails and read their texts... IF you want to. Just because you own a cell phone doesn't mean you have to let that tiny, demon-computer make you feel some sort of way, or make you feel some obligatory response sort of way. This is your choice completely, of course. You do what's right for you. You know you best. You know if this is helpful or not. But if you see my point and are hearing my plea, and if you don't want to do any of that social media stuff for a while, then don't. And don't feel bad about it. You are under no obligation to include anyone into your personal space of healing or moving forward or protecting your own energy. You *always* have a choice in what you want to say or not say and what you want to share or not share or what you want to hear or not hear. You owe no one anything right now.

Lastly, you may receive communication from people who *just don't get it*. When you do, let all that crap and all the crappy words flow right past you. **Reminder: you do not have to respond or engage with anyone. Isn't that fun?!**

That's the biggest divorce afterlife flex there is.

You don't have to tell anyone about any part of your divorce afterlife if you don't want to either—just as long as you know in your heart you *are* really healing and getting better in your thoughts and actions and you *are* genuinely feeling a sense of hope and happiness. You don't owe anyone an explanation for anything that has to do with your life; people do not need to know everything about your life at all, during a divorce or otherwise. Bottom line is: take a deep breath and make your decision about it. But ultimately, just log off.

The day that matters the most and the moment that matters the most is the one you're in.

CHAPTER THREE – INFIDELITY

———•⚜•———

Cheating. Adultery. Infidelity.

D ivorces happen all the time because of this. <u>For better or divorce</u> is what I think of when I think of a cheating spouse. The greener grass—the other side—we know that saying. It wasn't a surprise to me when I learned that lack of commitment and infidelity are the top two reasons for divorces these days. You don't say? Yup. They have been the top two and will probably remain the top two forever. I read somewhere that every 13 seconds, there is one divorce in America. That equates to 277 divorces per hour; 6,646 divorces per day; 46,523 divorces per week, and 2,419,196 divorces per year according to (www.wf-lawyers.com - divorce stats and facts). So, if those are the top two reasons for divorces, that's a whole lot of uncommitted little cheaters out there! Oof! Since it is such a common reason for divorces, I must speak on it because there is a really good chance that's the reason for your divorce. I implore you to read on, even if this does not apply to you.

The knowledge alone of a cheating spouse is very hurtful if you are on the receiving end. And knowing the dirty details of that infidelity can birth some really big insecurities in a woman—insecurities that sometimes take a lifetime to mend. You may know exactly how it feels to be a faithful and loyal person to a fault, and to have the one you love and adore cheat on you. And worse yet: the brief 'couple-dom' that took place doesn't last either (of course)! They rarely do last.

I have been on the receiving end of that hurt several times throughout my life, so I know the exact pain of being cheated on. And it can be the most painful thing that is attached to your already painful divorce. If you have felt this hurt, or are feeling this right now, you know that it hurts to the depths of your heart. Inevitably, you begin to look at yourself as if you were not good enough… or just *enough* of anything. You begin to look at yourself as though you need to change something about yourself in order to be more pleasing or more attractive or more experienced or different than what you are in some way. *More, more, more, better, better, better, whatever, whatever, whatever, etc.* In fact, you may have even heard of all the *things* you needed to "improve" on with yourself in order to have "deserved" or "kept" a faithful spouse from the mouth of the very same unfaithful spouse who put all those self-doubt bombs in your mind in the first place. What an excellent experience *rolling eyes back so far right now.*

That is all deflection, by the way. Those are all the deepest and biggest lies a woman will ever have to battle with when it comes to unfaithfulness in a marriage. That forced self-deprecation upon the one who got cheated on in order to relieve the guilt of the one who cheated. That's manipulative psychology 101—whereby self-confrontation or acknowledgement of the infidelity will never occur. It is a deflection from getting "too deep" with one's self hurtful behavior toward others. Classic cheater move. The cheater becomes the blamer or the victim themselves. This is the stuff that makes divorces really messy. This stuff makes cheating spouses want nothing to do with the "difficult" wife and kids because all the focus is now on the new, easy hoochie they have. This stuff makes people act just as angry as they feel. This stuff breaks my heart every time I hear it. And I've heard it a lot.

It is heavy hearted business—disloyalty—and I don't give a damn what kind of high divorce rate is out there at the time you are reading this; I don't care about the statistics surrounding divorces. I don't care that many people go through it and that is "just how life is" and there are "worse situations" out there. Yes, yes, we all haven't forgotten how to scale and measure all of life's misfortunes like that. I don't want <u>you</u> to care about the conditioning us women are receiving from the world where we are meant to feel like we are unworthy, unwanted, or less than after a divorce. Forget all of that. I want you to truly know that this is NOT what wives and mothers should have to accept and feel and experience in life because of an unfaithful husband!

Those numbers and statistics and the realities of the world we live in, with the amount of divorces that happen daily, does NOT lessen the stress, sadness, anger, and lost feeling that comes with this. It does not change the fact that it is really difficult for some people to ever feel really happy again or accepting of themselves after a divorce; especially when it involves infidelity. It does not lessen the larger and more challenging commitment to child rearing and parenting—that *one* parent will ultimately take on more of when all is said and done. James up the street may have cheated on his wife Julie, and Julie got over it and moved on. They may have each happily married other people the week after their divorce papers were signed, but that is not what happens a lot of the time when infidelity is in play. And that especially is not the case for most women because we bear most of the child rearing responsibility both within a marriage and then after a divorce.

And for a lot of us women, we are destroyed by a divorce because our life must now somehow magically just continue exactly like it was before, with all the responsibility but now do it with a shattered heart, okay?! Right. That circumstance kills off a lot of our self-love almost immediately. The last thing anyone probably wants to do is to think about a cheating spouse, accepting it fully, knowing that will never change and then just simply "press on." Those actions are hella hard. Even those intentions are hella hard! Hard because really accepting all of those things have a sort of finality to it. For things to be final, to a lot of us, there has to be a sense of closure (usually we like an apology of some sort).

There are wonderful stories out there of women who pick themselves up quickly and make a great life for themselves immediately, but that is not what a lot of us women do because we do feel so completely unvalued at the time of divorce. And that causes some real low self-esteem, thus: real slow movement forward. It's a deep well to climb out of as it is, and that extra element of unfaithfulness doesn't help any.

If you're in a situation where that sounds familiar and if you happen to be navigating through the woes of a cheating spouse, I hope you think about that perspective and give yourself a bit of grace in your thinking and feeling.

Okay, hear me real good now with what's to follow. In any circumstance of cheating or adultery, it is NEVER the fault of the one who got cheated on. Never ever. EVER. Do you believe that? I mean, really believe it? If you don't believe that with all your heart, are you willing to try? Do you know why you should believe that? Because, what the other person did to dishonor the commitment in the marriage had NOTHING to do with you. Say what now? *"I was cheated on, how does it have nothing to do with me?"* I hear you scream with an inside voice. One hundred percent, without a doubt, N O T H I N G to do with you. You were not the "cause" of anything. Yes, it happened *to* you, but it had nothing to do *with* you; as a person, a wife, a mother, a human—nothing.

We single-handedly make our own choices based on <u>who we are</u>—our character.

Yes, it is true. There is nothing you did or didn't do that *made* them do this or that or anything. There is nothing you could have or couldn't have done that *made* them do anything. There is nothing that you should have or shouldn't have done that *made* them do anything. That is not how it works in a marriage or in a relationship or in life—even though that is what we are force-fed to believe through all of tv and media. "What did I do to deserve that?" is a question that took me decades to release from my thinking. "I did not deserve that" is what replaced it. Try that on for size. See how that feels for you. **I did not deserve that**—say it out loud. Repeat that to yourself with the intention to fully accept it as complete truth with your current situation.

That type of decision, of infidelity, is made personally and singularly; one time or repeatedly. It doesn't matter the frequency or duration really. That decision has everything to do with *their* character. It has everything to do with *their* insecurity. It has everything to do with *their* immaturity. It has everything to do with *their* beliefs. *Their* nature. *Their* heart. It had nothing to do with you! I'd like you to really truly know this and believe this and not question any of your actions. Definitely don't question your appearance or your performance or your ability or anything that makes you the total of who you are. You're good just as you are. You don't need to change a thing, honey. That is never a reason to change something about yourself anyhow, right; because someone *else* says you need to.

Point is and point blank—you didn't deserve it. You didn't deserve disloyalty in your agreed upon commitment to one another, especially with responsibilities to that commitment that were so great. You did nothing wrong, and you are not the cause of how other people act! Re-read my words and receive my words on this. This takes a while to believe and accept, but work at it. Allow my perspective to be another choice you have at how you may heal.

That perspective about other people's yucky actions toward me not being *about me* was what I was missing in my early teen years, my early twenties, and even into my thirties. All that self-loathing on repeat every time someone found someone different. I'll never say "better," we don't do that in the here and now. But, different. I was so certain that I needed to change and warp and bend and morph into whatever it was I thought was pleasing in order to have someone love me enough to never cheat on me. I thought if I looked like A and acted like B and did C, that there should be no reason they would look elsewhere. I did that time and time again. And guess what? That never worked. DUH. It is really hard to break this cycle of thought though, because it is reinforced to us through the media. "That is what the problem is—us." That's totally backward! You know it is!

It takes so much more mindwork and soulwork than a woman should *ever* have to go through just to stop comparing ourselves to other women, especially the one your husband cheated on you with. Have you been there? Are you there right now? I'm sure you've had a heartbreak a time or two. But we're talking about infidelity and marriage, aren't we? There are huge commitments within this situation. And oftentimes, children. This adds a bit more to it all than just having that knowledge that you weren't the cause, dusting yourself off, swooping your kids up Wonder Woman-style and just walking away with your new, magically created, self-love club membership. There are *real* steep self-esteem ups and downs that are already happening if you're on the receiving end of that behavior, I know. There are some real big "baby steps" to take with the intention of moving forward from it. It's almost a forceful type of healing in a way, because you did nothing to deserve it, yet you HAVE TO deal with it on top of everything else. Oh, mama, do I ever feel you right now.

It all goes together, what I'm saying—whether or not you are divorcing for this reason or you know from previous experience. Since it is so common amongst divorce stories, I wanted to make sure you were seen, acknowledged, and reminded that you did nothing wrong and everything about you from the inside out, bottom to the top, is ALL good. Always has been.

Never question the value you have if your spouse stepped out on you. Other people's actions don't change the value of another person. That is the exact same thing you would tell your very own child if they were ever in the same situation, right? Of course. Likewise, that is the exact same thing you would remind a good friend or family member of if they had been cheated on as well, yeah? You would remind them of their high value as much as possible as they go through the tough emotions of it all, wouldn't you? The same thing applies directly to you. RIGHT NOW. Your good heart, your intelligence, your wit, your personality, your beauty, and your body are pretty amazing—and you are not lacking in any way. You must know and believe that there is no such standard of intelligence, personality, physique, beauty, or performance that one must stack up to or adhere to in order to be the "lucky recipient" of a faithful spouse. You know this as truth.

In every single divorce story that includes a cheating husband, I'm going to be so distastefully honest here; there would *never* have been enough handstand bj's, lovingly made 10-course dinners, nights out with the guys, hour-long oiled backrubs, perfectly ironed suits, subservient behavior, fitness model figure, or a supermodel face to ever have kept a husband from cheating on his wife. You know why? I know you do. It is because of all the things I already said. It simply has nothing to do with anything but the character of the cheating person! The external things, outside of the cheating person, ultimately have zero things to do with it! REALLY, really. People choose their own actions. People choose their own actions whether or not they even consider whose hearts will break because of those actions. People like to think that others cause them to cheat, but it is very much a singular action. This is one of those experiences in life that can hurt us the most because our hearts are involved romantically, which automatically involves every other part of us. Unfortunately, none of that is taken into consideration when we are dealing with someone who doesn't have a solid sense of self in place. That's how deeply broken women are created after divorce.

So, if you are sitting there relating to this situation of an unfaithful spouse, I see you. If you are sitting there and an unfaithful spouse is *not* your situation, be reminded here that we women have a plethora of things that test the love we have for ourselves every single day—including being cheated on—all the while conditioned to believe we are so damn different from one another. ALL women want to love themselves fully (*really* fully, not I'm-puttin'-on-a-front fully, like you know we do) and it is a lifelong struggle for most of us.

If you are still questioning where you may have "gone wrong" or did something wrong... I hope you feel my arm wrapped around you right now and you feel seen. I had that same thought a hundred times too, every single time I had been cheated on in my life. The fact of the matter is, and the answer to your question is—*nothing*. You did *nothing* to deserve it.

Say it: I DID NOT DESERVE IT.

You will once again feel confident in every area of your life. You will once again have super high self-esteem. And you will once again remember who you are and stand up straight and bask in that feeling of empowerment. This is in your future; this is where I am speaking to you from. You need to see these words so your mind knows that is a reality that is absolutely possible.

It takes a minute to recalibrate each area in your life that has been affected. And you're going to handle it with eloquence and remain in your confidence as a human who is going through something difficult. YOU ARE DEALING WITH A LOT. Take note of that right now. Everything feels heavy because it *is* heavy.

Look at the time you have spent taking care of, arranging, and managing others' lives! I hope you really know and understand the strength that was placed within the female psyche and spirit for times like these. Especially knowing that not all women will ever get to feel this particular strength in their lifetime. This strength is specific. You are a walking survivor because you are still standing and handling it. Don't like that term—survivor? Think that the word survivor should be reserved to just people who, say, survived cancer? Do you think it's too extreme of a term for someone who didn't "survive" something physical like that?

Look, I don't know everything, but I do know with absolute certainty that the emotional and mental toll that a divorce with children and infidelity takes on a woman is greatly underestimated because it happens so frequently. Do not downplay the severity of it all. Do not downplay the hurt in your heart. And do not downplay your huge role in this world as an amazing mother and human. Society wants you to feel like you gotta suck it up, sweetie. Don't listen to society. It doesn't know shit. You are surviving this. You are a survivor. Lean into the strength you do have by recounting how much you have contributed into making this a better world with your existence and love alone. You were created with a greater purpose beyond where you're at now. That greatness doesn't stop here.

CHAPTER FOUR - FORGIVENESS

We're going to take another look at forgiveness together, as adults, and reevaluate your thoughts on it while looking at the benefits it offers you. This will also help ease us up a little bit on our expectations of others and the disappointment that always follows when those expectations aren't met. The goal in this section is to gain an updated perspective on forgiveness and how it would help your healing if integrated into your daily mindset. We're not doing this because I think you lack the ability to understand and utilize forgiveness in your life already, but because we are on a self-love mission for you, and this obviously plays a big part in designing that mission in the best way.

If you feel like your ex-spouse is not deserving of your goodness and forgiveness right now, I absolutely hear you. I hear you so loud right now on that, it's as if you are yelling it directly into my ear canal. I hear you because sometimes husbands cheat... and never acknowledge it. I hear you because sometimes husbands abuse... and never say I'm sorry. I hear you because sometimes you discover husbands already have a whole other life and family... and when you find that out, they choose them instead. That is the hardest stuff to accept. That's so personal. I also hear you because practicing with forgiving the little things helps us in forgiving the bigger things.

There are many situations within a divorce where the expected mode of operation is to absolutely loathe the other person for anything and everything. No apologies for having those feelings and thoughts right now. If you are in the loathing mode and you know that—fine. That's understandable, especially when we feel wronged. I touched down on the loathing living bit for a bit, remember? But that can't last forever. It won't last forever. It really shouldn't last forever if you want to experience the purest happiness again. Right? I mean, it *could* last forever if you allowed it to, but I propose a better question and thought here—what does that do *for* you? Tell me one single benefit to you, and then you can just skip this part all together.

I'll start. Okay, okay, it *does* do something for you. I know exactly what loathing and hating does immediately. That's an easy one; it offsets our all-over-the-place-feelings and allows us to focus on just being mad as hell about everything. Okay, that relieves us short-term, like *really* short-term. But what will loathing and hating *eventually* do for you or to you? In terms of long-term benefits? And let's go further than that—what will the long-term benefits be for your children if you choose to loathe, hate, despise, or be mad as hell toward their other parent? Think about it, and then think about it again and again. You already know there is no benefit to that for anyone, despite it still being super duper hard to fully let go and forgive. I understand that, too.

I could four hundred bazillion percent reinforce and resuscitate your strong dislike or hatred for your ex until the end of time, no problem! I really could. I, and I want you to hear me good here, really extremely dislike liars, abusers, and cheaters who really don't even consider or give a damn about who they hurt. Extreme dislike. But not hate. See, it's incredibly easy for me to go there with you—to reaffirm your forgiveness-withholding hatred for the person and the circumstance that landed you here. That is the easiest thing to do, and that's what most of us choose. You can also find a group of people online to do that for you for eternity as well—keep you in the perpetual loop of hatred or resentment. Justification for your loathing can always be found. Justification for your hatred can always be found. You know that. But, from my own dirty work of holding onto extreme dislike, I have learned that the clean and clear soul and energy we all desire so deeply is always on the other side of forgiveness. You will never feel more cleansed and free in your mind and heart than in the moments you choose to forgive those who have hurt you and never apologized or even asked to be forgiven.

We can sometimes get pulled in the direction of reciprocating the same behavior that upset us. That, again, is so very human of us. An eye for an eye; you stab my back I'll stab yours is what encompasses that mode of thinking. Certain situations will cause this to happen throughout our lives, and it is all normal to have given in to that kind of thing in our younger years when we didn't know other ways to deal. But we know that doesn't sit right with us as adults, don't we? What we're choosing to do today though, is to move our minds far away from that mode, even though it is almost an automatic "defense" mode during divorce. Instead, we will move closer toward love and forgiveness. All of this is ultimately for your own benefit.

First of all, you must know that I cannot stand some of those old cliché quotes that we humans have adopted into our everyday vernacular. You know, the ones that are counterproductive in maintaining good health in our soul, spirit, and mind. And when these clichés float around the web like the little destructive demons they are, or are verbalized when we're communicating with one another— well, it makes my skin crawl. I know you've read this somewhere—it's the one that says, "The best form of revenge is forgiveness." That makes no sense. Neither does, "Kill them with kindness." Those are oxymorons, and I cannot stand them. They are low energy words with a low energy return when you invest your time into believing them; and it hurts my eyes tremendously every time I see them. Yet people use these "mantras" and "affirmations" as power statements or motivation, not knowing that it's really like a self-imploding mindset. How can one house the thought of revenge AND forgiveness in their being simultaneously? I'll tell you: one cannot do that. One cannot truly believe in forgiveness alongside a mind that believes in revenge toward the one who "did you wrong." Those players do not mix in the happiness game of life.

Now, do not misunderstand my sentiments here on what this revenge talk has to do with forgiveness, because hear this: I, being the sweet, kind-hearted and empathetic woman that I am, would absolutely do two life sentences in prison if someone ever harmed my children. Now, imagine the lengths in which I would have to go to that would get me a sentence like that. Right. That sounds like a whole lotta retribution and not a lotta forgiveness, Jenn. Okay, yes, I am human, and a mother, and I think like that, but I do not live with a vengeful spirit like that daily. That's not the "motivation" I recommend for you moving forward with things. Yet I understand how easy it is to grab onto that type of "toughening up" way of thinking, as it is a quicker type of temporary relief from the pain.

We hear that "We need to forgive ourselves before we can forgive others." Another cliché that we say. What on earth does that really mean? We hear and say the same crap so often, it really loses its luster and impact all together, doesn't it? But this platitude is different. This one has high frequency words. True words, even with its overuse. So how do you genuinely forgive yourself first? That's the first step, right? Well, yes, it really is. And it's actually the most beneficial to you immediately.

We are not entitled to any kind of nice, sweet, or fair treatment from anyone in any capacity, but we still have the hope that is what we'll all get. So, how about choosing that for our own self, first? Nice, sweet, and fair treatment toward us. It's a choice—a personal choice—to love and accept your entire being as a whole, knowing that we too have acted in ways that hurt others in our lifetime. That's the fair treatment part. I believe that the only way we can truly and continually forgive ourselves is the same way we can truly and continually forgive our children or our loved ones for upsetting us, hurting us, disappointing us, or letting us down in any way. I believe that is the simplest way to look at it.

We are often quicker to be gentle and easier toward someone we don't know or care about who may have done something toward us that we didn't like. But when it is someone we care about, trusted, or when it's even ourselves that may have bungled up a part of our enjoyable life experience, we have a tendency to shut down so we can dissect every portion of the offense and give it our own personal meaning of hurt.

So, let's back it up, dissect it, and take ourselves out of it for just a second. I want you to look at forgiveness from a perspective far away from the one you have right now. Below is something I penned out a few years after my divorce, and I'd like you to consider this perspective of forgiveness. It's not about divorce, it's not about you, and it's not about me. It's my own personal reflection on forgiveness with a specific storyline in mind. This is what I included in *my* reflection of forgiveness when I revisited its meaning to me as an adult—after divorce—just like I'm having you do. By the way, I absolutely name drop God and Jesus in this section, as I was thinking about the story of Jesus' crucifixion. Read on, whether you're a believer or not.

"I FORGIVE YOU... Kind of."

Have you been there in your mind and heart?

I have. Many, many times.

Forgiveness is this special kind of grace and understanding that follows a moment of learning and maturity. Forgiveness is there for us, because it is in our nature to mess up, to make mistakes, to err, to hurt people's feelings, to bungle it. That is part of humankind— behaving kinda poorly at times. It's what we have done, are doing, and will continue to do. What is not meant to be a part of us forever is the unreleased or unaccepted forgiveness attached to all those poor behaviors.

In our human existence, we know what feels right in our soul and we know what doesn't. There is a purpose behind the innate feeling of good and not so good. We are either moving toward or away from love. And because God is love, we feel it in our spirit because God's spirit is also in us.

I have said the words I forgive you and didn't mean it. Since I am using myself as an example here, I will also admit that I did not care or want to forgive at times either. Whether it was asked of me or not. I was absolutely aware of the affliction in my heart and mind thinking about an old situation or experience with other people but would have rather hidden the turmoil and fooled myself into thinking that just voicing the words themselves (I forgive you) had already done its good work in me.

In our world, these days, revenge and payback is often applauded and supported. I imagine we have all felt this way on some level—when someone or something affects us in a personal manner, either by actions or words, toward us or those we love. We are even troubled in spirit when we see wrongdoing on the other side of the planet with people we've never even met! For most of us, we want to see wrongs made right and for justice to be served. It's balanced and it's fair, and we like that kind of stuff. It's also because we all have good in us; it's because we all have a part of God in us, which is love.

I believe the human experience of forgiveness was designed to renew our souls and allow us to experience the other great things for our benefit... true happiness and love. I believe forgiveness was designed for us to also feel vulnerable and remind us we, too, are imperfect, and we make mistakes.

When we <u>ask</u> someone for forgiveness, we experience something within us that has already healed us, in a way. Even when we feel there are some mistakes that cannot possibly be forgiven, the story of Jesus asking God to <u>forgive</u> the very people who were crucifying him for no reason speaks so loudly to the power it has in our human existence. He was being killed... for NOTHING. He was without sin! He never made a mistake! And there he was, asking that his murderers be forgiven. I don't know about you, but if some fools were killing me and I hadn't done anything to these people, I wouldn't be asking for their pardon while they tortured me for half a day before my wrongful death.

You heard of forgive and forget, right? Well, we all know that doesn't really work for us humans either, right? Right. It just sounds like it's the easiest thing to do, and it sounds like we have our shit together when we say it.

Let's stop thinking that's a possibility and just put this reality in its place:

The art of forgiveness isn't mastered overnight. Art, you say? Yes. I say art. Why? Because forgiveness looks, feels, and means different things for each individual, much like art. Forgiveness takes on many different forms over our lifetime, and it also takes time itself. The more experiences we have with it, the more we can see it is needed to complete our unique life picture we are all painting with every action, word, and deed.

Forgiveness isn't about waiting for someone else to say they forgive you when you ask for forgiveness either. See, when it comes to the "I'm sorry" and the forgiveness, it is never about what the other person has to say in response. It is where <u>you</u> are at in your own heart with it, and with the love you have for yourself.

Let's say that the person that you need to forgive has passed away... see where the apparent problem is there with leaving the finality of the forgiveness experience with them? How can the audible "forgiveness exchange" come from someone who cannot speak? It can't. We are not to wait on someone handing over verbal acceptance of our apology or hearing their apology for forgiveness to be official. It's rather incredible that forgiveness, from soul to soul, can travel across different times in history! When you apologize and ask someone else to forgive you, they may say they don't forgive you. What then? Are you then locked into your guilt and mistakes forever? NO! You are already changed and free, in a way, when you ask to be forgiven in the first place or you extend that grace toward someone else.

When we willingly let our thoughts and our heart enter

into this vulnerable state and we welcome that feeling of vulnerability and the process of moving forward, we are again reminded of love. When practicing the art of forgiveness, we accept our vulnerability and actually announce it to someone else! And there is absolutely no faking this experience.

The beautiful art of forgiveness looks and feels different for everyone, but it all comes with the option of freedom, if you want it. ALWAYS CHOOSE FREEDOM. See, bitterness and anger, revenge, karma, retribution, even hate toward someone else, will never ever actually affect them... but will always affect you. And yes, I know you've heard that cliche a hundred times too—so cheers to making it to 101!

You do not have to be religious or a believer of anything to actually grasp onto that part in Jesus' story and the concept of forgiveness and the love surrounding it. Jesus' death alone shows the depth in which forgiveness can reach our soul and the value in which he knew it had. Wow. Yearning to feel love rather than hate is very much in your DNA, which makes it apply to you no matter what your religious or non-religious standing is. We innately know that love is the way to go, because it feels great and it makes our thoughts great, and forgiveness is a form of love. And it's a special kind of love for self when you choose to forgive others, even when it includes very adult circumstances sans apology from the offender.

At this perfect timing in your life, where you are

learning to give your life new meaning and direction, you are capable of refreshing and updating your stance on this whole forgiveness thing too. Reading the high energy words below can and will refresh your mind.

- I choose to forgive my own self for all the things that I am holding onto in my heart.
- I am loving myself when I choose forgiveness in any form.
- I choose to think loving things about who I am right now and allow forgiveness to be a part of who I am.
- I am choosing to be a forgiving person with every choice I make.

True forgiveness is hard to come by these days because it seems our crazy culture backs up the *living for numero uno* mentality. And while I do want you to focus on just taking care of yourself right now, you can absolutely still do that as you remember that forgiveness is a gift to your *own* soul when you are releasing expectations and forgiving others. We are often misguided in the direction of being hard with those who do us wrong, as to "protect" ourselves from people doing that to us again. But that isn't protection from anything. That's continual exhaustion from energy put in the wrong place. Hardening your heart takes energy—energy to do the opposite of what comes natural to us; to love one another. At this time in life, you're going to be exhausted already, so try to choose love and forgiveness at every turn—even if it's hour by hour and minute by minute. And not even necessarily FOR others, maybe just focus on forgiveness with the realization of the way ALL humans can all behave rather poorly toward others sometimes.

Being stiff, too self-controlled, and shut off to acknowledging that some forgiveness needs to take place is tough on our spirit. So much. You can reset forgiveness mode five times in a row if you need to. These actions are the things that will make a difference in your upcoming days. Giving ourselves that gift of grace and forgiveness for any and everything, every day, really allows the other good stuff to flow naturally. The forgiveness for others flows naturally. The acknowledgement for the severe and the softer "offenses" to us becomes easier to do, and then easier to release into the wild. Being intentional in choosing to love yourself through the whole, entire history of you, the present you and the future you, is exactly what a forgiving person does. That's you—an incredibly strong, smart, discerning, understanding, expectation-releasing, and forgiving person.

"To Err Is Human; To Forgive, Divine"

—**Alexander Pope**

CHAPTER FIVE – DIVORCE DECREES AND CHILD CUSTODY

———•❦•———

Have you ever known two people divorcing and having a party with their friends about it, celebrating their decision to just go back to being friends (or strangers) and not married? I haven't known anyone like that. I'd like to think that those people and their decision to marry in the first place was made at the little white chapel in Vegas just hours after they met one another at the bar and right before they both puked up all that overpriced tequila they drank together. Because celebrating a divorce isn't the norm. Especially when there are children involved. Some real deep feelings come out when a divorce involves children. Some real deep feelings come out when a divorce involves children and money. Some real deep feelings come out when a divorce involves children, money, and infidelity. Some real deep feelings come out when a divorce involves children, money, infidelity, and pets. One of those factors, or any combination of them, can cause a divorce to be anything but a celebration, messy even. But is there another way to make it less messy with some of those factors? Yes, of course. Simplicity is key. In this section, we're going to travel through some thoughts and perspectives when it comes to decision making with the divorce and the custody arrangements, and the realities of living out those first moments of the actual arrangements you agreed on.

Okay, you'll know right away whether or not you'll be able to manage filing for divorce yourselves without legal intervention and mediation. I can tell you right now that if you have a home to sell, debts, vehicles, boats, pets, children, savings, investments, or a prenup, you will be better off lawyering up. If you couldn't communicate with your spouse or see eye to eye on the majority of things before, you will absolutely not want to try to do it now without professional guidance. That would be like trying to roast a turkey and bake an apple pie for the first time ever on Thanksgiving Day—probably just sit down. Lawyers are spendy, and if you didn't hate them before, you'll probably hate them after this when you see how much they make from your divorce alone. But that guidance through the hundred billion documents that are needed to settle a divorce properly, while you feel like dogshit, is such welcomed relief and therefore makes it kinda priceless. A complicated marriage with a lot of components—like, for example: children—becomes a complicated divorce with a lot of components. That is a fact. That makes jogging into a lawyer's office real easy for the lot of us, no matter what they're charging.

Whatever the driving force is behind your decision to involve a legal team or not, trust your choice. Don't look anywhere but directly ahead or directly at your lawyer and tell them what you want for you and your kids and why. This part matters. You don't have to accept what your lawyer thinks is best for you if it doesn't feel right to you. Trust yourself and speak from your heart. Now, if there are personal circumstances of abuse or substance abuse or unhealthy living conditions—that is another story, and you need to make those decisions based on your own beliefs and with a lawyer's recommendation. Always trust your own gut feelings and intuition with regard to your situation.

Okay, so you have a lawyer. Great. This is a huge opportunity for you to transfer half of your stress to them. Get your money's worth and let them do what they are there to do, which is guide you through everything that needs to be done. Let go of the wheel with this one! You are not doing this on your own; that's a relief. Take it off your list for things you're completely responsible for right now. Put a bit of faith in the expertise of who is representing you.

In the case of divorce proceedings, some spouses want to "drag the other through the mud." My dad once told me that his lawyer recommended doing that to my mom when they were filing for divorce, which he declined because he didn't think like that because he's not a prick—thank God! But it's true; some spouses want to take advantage of the other spouse, to remain in "control" of things. Yes, even during the divorce, folks. Some spouses want to just move on and agree to whatever shit agreement is thrown out there, too, which produces a lot of animosity from ex-wives because it seems as though the father doesn't give a crap about actually parenting the kids. Some spouses care about everyone's well-being and will be there for you and your kids through it all and will have the best, most open communication throughout the whole thing (who are you people, by the way?). Some spouses quickly agree to a $30k a month child support payment plus alimony (again, who are you people?!). That's certainly not my story. Probably not yours either. Either way though, how it was in your marriage working together usually predicts quite accurately how it *will be* working together through the divorce paperwork, as well as in any future decision making regarding the kids and custody. Now, if that part has already passed—signing the paperwork—then you know exactly what I'm saying. You worked together just as well as you had always worked together, or not. You may have signed things quickly just to do it and be done.

And that's okay. You do what you have to do through this whole thing; you trust yourself and your decisions, and it's all good.

If you're headed into the mediation and proceedings, here's some perspective on what you can expect or prepare for. As I said earlier, the more components there are, the longer the proceeding will take. There is the division of assets and debts, if any, and the deciding and dividing of the contents of the home. Possibly selling the home and where proceeds will go, debt responsibilities, credit cards, joint accounts, vehicle responsibility, insurances, investments, savings, IRA's, 529's, moving costs, where animals go if any, and child support and possibly alimony. I know there's so much more, but I think that list did just fine with the overwhelm. One of the things that is underestimated when you are getting a divorce and you are using lawyers is the amount of time and energy one must invest into it. No one wants to dredge through 3-9 months of divorce proceedings, but that is generally what it takes. Yuck. The 6-month cool off period is also a law in some states. Which is essentially a 6-month minimum before a divorce can proceed to filing, allowing the couple to reconcile, if possible, within that 6-month timeframe. I imagine that was put into place because the *most* real communication ever had between a husband and wife sometimes only happens during divorce proceedings! That's ample time to think over and discuss some important things on purpose because it is literally hours and hours and hours of mediation time. So, be prepared for all that, and try your very best to be honest with yourself about *why* you are making the decisions that you are making with regard to the divorce itself and the custody. Avoid making decisions based on and in correspondence to how you are hurting or believe *they* hurt you. Avoid that at all costs! If it is truly 3-9 months of this— that thinking and energy will be detrimental to your entire being. More on that to come.

Be bold with your voice if you have 100% conviction that your ex is not making the best choices or suggestions on behalf of your children. That is truly what all that back and forth in the meditation is based on, you know. Finding the most agreeable and least disruptive forward movement for everyone, especially the children. For example, if you were a stay-at-home-mom, the logical arrangement is for you to continue to care for the children like you did, but now with child support and alimony. So, a bit of the pressure of finances is taken off, so as to not completely disrupt what the environment was like for your children before. That's not selfish. That's what is most logical and most beneficial for the children. Same with household items—decisions on this stuff should be based on the reality of who can replace these things easily and who will need the things immediately so as to not disrupt the environment where the children will spend the majority of the time at first. You've heard that other bs thing out there in the world that I've heard too, of the wife taking the husband "to the cleaners" during a divorce, or vice versa. In fact, there are actually a hundred different articles on that very thing if you Google that term right now. It's appalling to read. Yuck. But look at this with logic. Those arrangements are not made out of spite, most of the time, but rather, from a place of accepting that life is moving forward and there is a need for a realistic approach on behalf of and for the stability of the children and their environment. The one who has the most responsibility with caring for the children at first should not be stripped of all the things needed to support that responsibility... that is absolutely a surefire way to make it a stressful environment for your own children to be in.

Bigger Picture:

A sound mind and heart are desperately needed when making decisions about child custody and having that "child-like" vision of what *they (the children)* will experience during and after the divorce. This is so important; yet can be extremely difficult when going through a divorce, I know. Whether you are just getting started on it, are in the middle of it right now, or you know what it all entails because you just got through it, know that whatever final decisions or agreements that will happen or happened were the ones that made the most sense at the time you made them. Do not question yourself. Give yourself a break and exhale every time you feel like you're not making the "right" choices. There are only a few things that are ever really set in stone in this lifetime; a child custody order is not one of them. You can revisit later, but for right now, just breathe out and trust yourself with any decision you made, are making, and will make!

Whichever way you think it should go with who will have the majority of custody and responsibility, make it work for you and your individual situation, even if you are lawyered up. You CAN write or suggest your very own proposal of what you want the agreement to look like. I did. After thinking about what was best for our situation and for our children and with my sister doing her research, I proposed a "hybrid" agreement where we would have the standard stuff in there with split time with them as best we could, even being a state apart, and the hybrid portion was for their father to have the ability to come visit them as much as he could or wanted. Now, if those options and suggestions are ever used is a different story, but the main point and purpose with it is—it was there. It was an open agreement to support and maintain an ongoing relationship with a parent and child without a big hiccup. It wasn't just a "standard" approach or the easy fill-in-the-blanks agreement or what agreement worked easiest and best and fastest for the expensive as hell lawyers. Nope. It wasn't *for* the lawyers. It wasn't *for* me. It wasn't *for* him. It wasn't *for* ease. It was <u>for the kids</u>. I wanted them to be available for the health of that relationship. That is what a parent does when they love their children so much... they see the bigger life picture as if they were looking through the eyes of their children. And what those eyes see are two parents and all they want is love from both of them and time with both of them.

If you are working toward an amicable divorce, and you and your ex seem to be working okay together so far—that's so good. Amazing, in fact. That is so hard these days. You know this. Keep that healthy mindset and momentum going just as you have been. If you wish that is how it was going with your ex right now, keep trying and keep in mind that you can always revisit your decisions later if they're not working or things change. The most important part is to try and choose—together—the most "non disruptive to your children" route. Your kids will feel all the love they need to feel at a time like this, and that picture should remain the driving force in your every decision, forever. No matter how hard. Step back and back and back—the bigger the picture, the better. The bigger the picture, the simpler it is.

Okay, where is my sassy pants momma who wants to punch my face with all that unrealistic harmonious bullshit? You may be rolling your eyes so hard right now thinking that there is no freakin' way you will be able to play fair and be amicable because you already know your soon to be ex-spouse won't play fair or be amicable. Or you may be thinking what a complete incompetent fool he is. Or you may be thinking that you'd rather chop off your arm than to cater to his requests or suggestions or agree to anything that looks slightly "better" for him and his life than you and your life, especially after what he's done. I hear you. Ooohh, I hear you my little, sassy sister. I know this is going to be so very much to ask of you when you're in the feelings you're in. I know, because when it comes to child custody situations, I have experienced all sides of thinking, feeling, and acting—with *and* without logic, ego, trust, and faith. I know because I, too, like fairness. I like when people play nice. I like when people can think about others before themselves. I like it when people are honest. I like competence. I like accountability and shared responsibility. And I love my children with all of my whole heart. You too, right? Of course! If that's where you're at, I can only ask that you reach for your faith… create some new faith… or borrow some faith from someone right now in that you and your former spouse are able to work together harmoniously at some point with all of this.

"Leap of faith – yes, but only after reflection"

—**Soren Kierkegaard**

Okay, we're jumping into some other real experiences and perspectives, and the sentence right after this one is a heavy hitter—so, brace yourself. **Your divorce will affect your children.** Oof. Knowing and accepting this truth about what's ahead for your children, and feeling what you are feeling in the depths of your soul every time you think of it, likely makes you want to curl up in a ball and cry for the rest of your life. Extreme, you say? Nah. Totally expected. I felt like the worst human being on the planet with that knowledge. I felt like a terrible mother when I thought of it, and I also felt such animosity toward my ex at the same time. *He was a part of it too!* I would scream in my own thoughts. *Why am I the one that has to do most* *of the soul repairing and explaining to the kids and possibly be blamed for this since I'll be with them the most?!!* I had never felt that life was more unfair than I did in those moments of thought. I felt as if God wasn't near me and my broken heart. *I did my best... I was a good mother, right? I'm still a good mother, right?* I asked myself while I sobbed. I'm crying right now as I write this; because during the custody mediation, I know you will, at least once, question your entire existence as a good mother when it comes to this part too.

All we want to do is protect our children from the stuff that will hurt them, and look where we are now. *That thought is what crushes every wonderful mother out there when it comes to their children and divorce.* All of these thoughts are unavoidable. So, let's deal directly with some of them right now, head on. Okay, so divorce *will* affect them negatively somehow, and it may carry well into adulthood. Okay, that's the extreme of it! You just heard it. No more letting the mind wander over how this will possibly affect them and for how long. We just don't know all that. What we do know is; it's a possibility. So with that, you'll do your best with your decisions today and the decisions to come. You can cry as much as you need over that truth. I did. And I still do some days. I'm still doing my best, just like you. You are an excellent mother!

As a mother, we will feel the sting of divorce and how it changed the landscape of ours and our children's lives for years to come. Even when we're all happy and just fine!

That's because change affects people, and this is a change. We will feel and remember the life changing effects forever because we care so deeply and instinctively. Our nurturing nature as a "full time" mother is being cut short, and we know it. This part changes us. This part changes them. This part changes us where we now might feel deeply inadequate to ever "handle a marriage" again, and further, ever "handle our own kids" or even "know our own kids" the way we hoped to and were designed to. These millisecond thoughts will tempt us over and over again to replace faith and hope with sadness and anger. These thoughts sometimes tempt us into raking our exes over hot coals during divorce and custody proceedings too, because it is **just not fair**.

You're going to choose what you choose, but I'm hoping you do understand and see that these thoughts are based off of the hurt in your heart and the love that you have for your children. We want them to feel okay, and at a time like this, we are unable to do that for them, and that's painful.

The paperwork is soul work. There is a lot of learning when it comes to this process of the "paperwork" of your divorce. You will most definitely learn a few things about yourself while you're dealing with this step in the whole thing. One thing you might learn really quickly as you start looking over split custody arrangements is that you really may not trust him to take good care of them like you do. Brace yourself again—this one's going to hit hard too—he won't. He will not care for them like you do. He is going to care for them like *he* does. He may not even continue to do that or want to in the future; take care of them. Whoa, what? Pretty scary thought, isn't that? Yeah, that *is* a possibility of what could happen. And we just shot that scary thought down just by saying it. I have a few friends who have divorce afterlife stories of just that. Where the father chose another life and another family, other than the first one he created. He is not present in the lives of his first set of children. It's maddening and it makes me so angry on behalf of the beautiful children who are on the receiving end of that kind of crappy situation. So, if that's *your* situation, you all did not deserve that, and I am so sorry you are hurting in that way. Also, I love you. If that's not your situation right now, be ever so grateful that the other parent wants to have involvement and responsibility right now, even if you don't think he'll do as good a job parenting them as you do. You must allow that, and support that as much as you can, on behalf of your children. You know your situation, and you know your gut feelings on all of this. Listen to YOURSELF on this. Listen to your LOVE with this. Do right by your kids when it comes to all of this.

See, *we* cannot control anybody. We cannot control the kind of care, fairness, or even involvement we would like to see. *Even involvement?* Yes. That's the bottom of the barrel for some divorce afterlife stories out there. No involvement with the children, no support, monetarily or otherwise. Completely gone. Oof. Which means this whole chapter and divorce decrees and child custody orders literally doesn't even apply to some situations out there. It happens like that every single day! I see you too. I cannot even try to understand what you're feeling. But I see you. You are way stronger, in a very different sense than I am.

We cannot expect or count on anyone to replicate who *we* are, as mothers, and how we care and how we raise and how we love our own children. Your ex will do that in their own way. This is where huge faith is born or borrowed and lots of prayer or meditation comes in. This is where keeping your mind busy or staying active in doing what *you* love comes in. This is where therapy comes in. This is where time with friends and family comes in. This is where journaling or video journaling comes in. This is where music and art come in. This is where talking with other divorced people comes in. You will need an array of happiness producing distractions and actions in order to combat the expected roller-coaster-rock-bottom emotions surrounding this part. This part and this change take time to move through because it is multi-faceted with respect to our different circumstances, and it is very much ongoing as long as we're breathing. This change is one of the more difficult ones for us moms. Expect it. Prepare for it. Breathe through the waves of it one breath at a time.

The first time without them and the first holiday without them is going to hurt. In those first moments when you exchange your children for the first time with your ex and you get in your car and leave—without them—you'll need your support system lined up and available to chat with you or meet up with you so you can work through those initial pangs of separation. This will not feel like a usual mommy time break away from your kids. You'll feel the difference with the first exchange.

What I want you to do right now is picture me. Picture me in your mind during the first child exchange with my ex-husband. It was the first time they would not be in my care, or even nearby me, and also was the longest time we were ever apart. That first official exchange. We each drove a few hours to meet in the middle of our separate states so the children could finally go spend time with their dad at his home, after being with me since the divorce. For those two hours of driving with them, I did not cry. I don't remember what the hell I did in those two hours, but I know I didn't cry. I know I looked at them a hundred times in my rear-view mirror though, wanting to cry. The time out of the car getting suitcases in trunks, saying hellos and goodbyes was brief, and then I was waving goodbye to them as they sat on the other side of the car window, waving back at me as it pulled away from me going in the opposite direction of where I was going. Tears immediately started falling down my cheeks at a pace that I can say I've never felt tears fall down before. Tears were in my eyes the entire two-hour drive home as I prayed to God, asking why divorce had to be a part of my life story. I actually screamed that question... out loud... several times as I gripped my steering wheel so tightly, because I wanted the pain to leave my body somehow. I wasn't nice about it. *How would my heart handle not being able to protect them and raise them like a mother should be able to*, I thought over and over. I was so angry that *this* was what I had to feel for the rest of my life... I was someone who *already* had a very sad heart to begin with! That is what it was like for me. That first exchange. That first separation from them hurt. That moment was tough. It will be for you too. Maybe not in the same ways, but in some way.

My purpose with that was for you to be reminded of moments like that existing... thoughts like that existing... feelings like that existing... experiences like that existing... women like that existing out there. You are not, and will not be, alone with your first or twenty-first exchange. And I promise you, your thoughts will not be the same on your ninety-first exchange as they were on your first. I'm right there with you.

How can you prepare for it??

When you know you're going to be without your kids for the first time and every time after that, I have found that you will feel a whole lot better if you plan to do as many things that fill your happiness and contribution tank as you can. Being without them will be a big adjustment to your purpose-meter as a mother when you don't have any actual mothering to do. Yup, it feels *just* as crappy as it sounds. It may be like that for the first entire year of exchanges! I would get into my car and lose it after they drove away. Then, my crying at exchanges lessened, but the prayers for their safety and happiness increased. Of course, I still prayed with the same questions asked about why people's lives really had to feel like this and be like this, but I tried my best to prepare my heart better for the next time and the next.

You know this stuff is coming—this is YOUR preparation guide—this is your preliminary pep talk for accepting the stuff that you'll just naturally think because you're a mom. Your mind might spin up a thousand different scenarios about how they aren't going to be buckled in properly, or at all, and how they are probably going to be exposed to a bunch of hoebags, drugs, foul language, and a whole lot of garbage conversations that won't teach them a single positive thing about life, and they'll be addicted to alcohol and cigarettes by the time they return to you next week. On that first exchange, your mind might even have them dead and buried before nightfall. Your mind really might go there! Those are real thoughts! I had them all! Oh no, is my motherhood showing? Alright, you may not go there in your mind like I did (and still do sometimes). If not, REJOICE! And, again, I say rejoice! But if it does spin off... it's expected... and okay. You'll get better and better at bringing it back into peace and trust.

The first big holiday or your favorite one to spend with them, and all other special days (like birthdays) without them, or splitting up those days, will be tough. And just like with the first exchange, you'll feel the difference, even when you're surrounded by the rest of your entire family whom you also love. The feeling on these special days and holidays without them hasn't changed for me still; it's tough every time, but I offer the perspective I have with it now... any day when you're together and happy becomes a special day, and you can celebrate whatever holiday or birthday you want to celebrate together on whatever day of the year you want. You will look forward to making every single minute that much more special with them. I know that sounds so far off from where you might be at in your mind with it right now. As I am re-reading it again, it sounds grossly cliché, like, "there's a pot o' gold at every rainbow's end!" and I'm actually not sure if I even want to keep that in this book; because reading stuff like that when I'm sad has actually made me feel like shit somehow! But, I am speaking to you from your future, remember? So, all I see is your happy heart and your children's happy hearts and your loud laughter and your wonderful moments of peace together. All of that is in the making; you'll get there. And again, you're an excellent mother. (Just in case you didn't fully take that in a moment ago.)

As I learned more about myself through the divorce proceedings and after it was finished, I got a few reality checks as well. It's going to happen; embrace that truth! A big reality check I had when they were away from me was the reality of this control thing I had going on. We mothers control lots of things—most of the things that have to do with our children's lives. That's just a big part of motherhood. I had control of the kids. I had control of the kids within the home. I mostly had control of the home. I loved it. It was safe and secure for my insecure heart. Turns out, control was the *only* thing that made my heart feel safe and secure. That was the only thing that did it! Nothing else made me feel safe and secure in my life like control did. It was the home and me protecting the kids at home. That is the only thing I felt I had control of in my entire being. And now, I had no "control" over any of that; or them. *That* was the core of my fear. That was one of the biggest emotional wounds I had. I didn't control the environment for them any longer. I didn't control how they were going to consume the world any longer. As a mother, I would not be present to oversee how different and possibly damaging that other parenting style, that wasn't mine, might be for them... and there was nothing I could do about it! That is hard to accept as a mom. From the very first time they were away from me and with him, and every other time after that, I was only in control of me, and one half of the environment that they would be raised in. I had no choice *but* to accept that. That was a reality check I wasn't ready to receive.

That realization and the actual acceptance of it didn't happen in the same day, by the way. Of course it didn't. Anything that provides us with an opportunity of "letting go" of something to learn something requires a whole lot of forced uncomfortableness. Those opportunities are hard to see and equally hard to absorb on the first go. In fact, I still don't see a lot of them as opportunities at all when they're right in front of me! That was definitely a process that I had a lot of struggle with. With that struggle came my pride of motherhood, anger that I had no control, and resentment toward my ex for all that, with a bit of bitterness on the side for good measure. Okay, actually more like a shit ton of bitterness. I feel like such a human being right now with all this human emotion honesty, it's crazy.

And here we are—you and I—together in our shared experience of divorce.

I know you know people who have used kids like pawns when it comes to child custody. I know you've heard the stories. I've heard them too. I know you have that one friend where it's a nightmare of a custody situation and has been a nightmare for over a decade. I have that friend, too. No one ever "wins" like that. No one enjoys life like that. No one loves like that. I know you know that as truth. What a divorce teaches you right away is that you *still* have to be a part of the decisions for your children and for yourself; that will finalize the custody and divorce decrees, no matter how much or how little you believe you and your spouse can work well together.

Life *still* goes on during your divorce (your life, too!). Your motivations, intentions, and approach to the decrees and arrangements have everything to do with how *you* will feel, which will play into how your kids will feel. Focus not on the yuckiness of the divorce proceedings (because it will feel yucky the entire time), but rather focus on your spirit and mind and your ability to be amicable, despite every terrible thing that could have happened leading up to where you are now. In this context, and to me, amicable means you are not "out to get" the other person, because you know darn well there are children involved, and whatever affects the parent will affect the child, in essence. Decisions that are the least disruptive to the life of the child(ren) is the baseline understanding to make amicable happen in divorces. People are generally amicable during all this when both are using that logic. But when this logic is not used, it usually falls into the category of "battling it out." Meaning there is someone winning and someone losing. God help us all.

It is saddening to see the ruthlessness that is encouraged when a divorce is taking place. "Winning in a divorce" is the silliest thing I have ever heard in my entire life, yet I have heard it in all forms of media *and* in real life. No one wins in a divorce. As such, "getting back" at your spouse for the things they did or didn't do in your marriage via divorce proceedings and custody hearings is one of the biggest wastes of time on the planet. Not to mention, it's cruel, and is just plain not good for your well-being in general.

Your opportunity to have more love-filled days than hate-filled days during the divorce and in your divorce afterlife, and in your numbered days here on earth, is by remembering you can choose which way you want to try to feel in every single moment.

What's the bigger picture here? Ask yourself that often to keep yourself in check, or when you hit a roadblock in coming to any understanding or agreement, now or in the future. The bigger picture here *is* and *always will be*: "What will *they* (the kids) experience with the choices and arrangements you both are making?" Please *do not* forget the bigger picture while you are sitting in a lawyer's office with all your stress and away from your kids. Because the moment you take *them* out of the equation, you are left with your very specific adult feelings that you want nothing more than to reciprocate to the one who brought them out. YOUR PERSONAL HEALING WILL NOT HAPPEN WITH THAT MINDSET, and neither will a healthy child custody plan.

I didn't do this myself, but maybe even print out a few pictures of your child/ren and give one to your ex so you both have one in hand as you go over the final all-our-love-for-the-children decisions. Then, try with all your might to choose those—*together* if you can. If you're past that part and you think this would help with things going forward—try to communicate this to your ex. Trying to think better or different about all of this can really lead to some peace that you didn't think you could have under these circumstances.

What you owe to yourself right now is to be amicable, because it is natural for you to want to feel good in your decision making, to trust your own judgment, your intelligence, and your communication skills in what you want and why you believe it's best for you and your children. That will benefit *you* in the depths of your own amazing, loving soul. It will also benefit your children more than you can fathom right now.

You're not doing any of this amicable stuff for the appearance of being an "amicable wife" in the divorce. You don't give a shit about that. You give a shit about your own personal experience and feeling—that is what you are nurturing right now. You trust yourself here. You trust God. You trust the universe. Trust that this will all work out, and trust that being amicable, despite some messy marriage circumstances, doesn't mean you're a weak pushover and you're dismissing the messy stuff as acceptable to you. No. It means you are tapping in to the strongly confident woman and mother you are, who is standing completely upright in her high value and believing that this approach is healing your heart with every sound choice you make.

As I was filling out the dreaded divorce paperwork, I did not decide to change my last name back to my maiden name. I didn't want to think about much during that time. I didn't want to spend any more money. I had always just thought it was like thousands of dollars and a whole lot of hassle. I also didn't want to feel as if I was cutting the name-tie with my children somehow; all I wanted was to just be closer and closer to them right then because of all the changes. Having a different name from them would have felt like a direct hit to my fragile heart, and of my own doing. I didn't want to cry again. So, I quickly marked no and moved on.

See, there are a lot of divorced moms who keep the ex's last name for those exact reasons. My mom did. Some women keep that last name so school staff or others will not question the differentiating last names between them and their children. They keep the last name because they don't want to spend the money and deal with the not-so-easy process of updating all the connections they have with the old name. They keep the last name because they operated in their career as such and don't want to have to "re-brand" and re-do and re-introduce themselves. Some keep the last name because that is how people "know" them. Some keep the last name because they like it better than their original. Some keep the last name to be connected to their ex-spouse in a way. And some keep the last name because that's just what they have seen so many others do. Any choice is all okay and acceptable and personal to each of us. But let me offer a perspective into why I finally chose to go back my maiden name.

For me, the time wasn't right to decide on the name change when I was filling out divorce paperwork. And even though I thought about it before, when I finally joined the working world, it seemed like too much work, and it wasn't worth the time or money to me. But even then—knowing there was going to be "branding" in my business—I, reluctantly, put my old married name on everything. I even got into the annoying habit of telling people that was my "married last name" even though I was, in fact, divorced now. That is how much I didn't want to have it (my married last name) that I literally explained this to people who DID NOT ASK for all that information! It's rather funny thinking about how all that extra time was devoted to me explaining this to people who didn't give a crap about it like I did.

So, I moved through the world for three years with that old last name, knowing I hated it, and yet did nothing about it. Goodness gracious, the lengths we go to in order to avoid shit we don't want to deal with, much like spending three minutes emptying the dishwasher. It was far easier to just not think about it than it was in changing it, I thought. We do that, don't we. Go for easy, but miserable—comfortable but crappy. But as time went on, and more "old married name explanations" flew out of my mouth, I realized I truly hated using a last name that I really did not desire to be associated with any longer. I thought about it constantly, with every interaction I had and with every piece of paperwork I filled out. For some reason, it still made me feel like the weakling I thought I was in my marriage. It made me feel incapable and small. Like someone had their thumb on little ole me. The name felt like the thumb. Like I had no identity other than the one I used to be married to. That was not my name anymore. My original last name was better suited for me anyhow. My original name, the name that had the original awesome parts of me attached to it, was the one I preferred.

So, after three and a half years had already passed in my divorce afterlife, one night in casually conversing with a friend about the divorce, we ended up on the topic of my last name. My friend said something to the effect of, "You are obviously getting back to YOU and that is a significant part—your last name... and your original last name is way better for you!" He was so right. I had thought about it for so long. I had thought about it as I introduced myself to loads of people over the years, and cringed inside every time, as it never felt like I was introducing the *me* that I was now. I thought about it in the sense of no one really seeing the growth in me—the stronger, more confident woman I was now after struggling so privately after the divorce.

So, the morning after the conversation I will never forget, I went online to see about changing it back... and decided to do it... that day. I decided to get my last name back no matter the cost or time. I was prepared to finalize all the effort I put in to rebuilding myself up to standing with confidence in myself, by getting my actual name back. I was choosing to let it signify something that was important to me within my divorce afterlife. And I knew that would be the only paperwork in my adult life that I wasn't going to read over before signing! My decision was made.

How hard was it to change it back? What did it cost? I hear you say.

Get this. It took three pieces of paper, two signatures,

$124 dollars and 10 minutes at my local circuit courthouse with a free notary. That's right, folks. THAT is what I avoided for over three years. Unbelievable. I have never felt more ME than the day I walked out of there knowing that in just one week, I would have an official document stating my last name was restored to its original. I would now walk this earth like the proud owner of the identity that was gifted to me by my very own parental units. The identity in which came full circle (but with more love!) after such a painful divorce.

The only thing that I ever thought about it was moms just keeping the same last name as the kids for whatever personal reason they had. Mostly, I believe, because maybe moms didn't want to be judged as some sort of floozy who just had a child with someone but were never actually married to them. A different last name will do that sometimes, you know. Us women, we have accepted some pretty weird, and unfortunately society-supported, delusions that we're loose, morally unsound individuals if we have different last names than that of our offspring. Welp, I am here to tell you, that shit doesn't matter in the grand scheme of things. It really doesn't. I promise.

If you feel like you want to change your name back, change your last name back immediately, honey! The married last name will NEVER have anything to do with the real connection you and your children have. It severs nothing. Listen, you need to hear the choices you have when it comes to your divorce, not just do what your family or friends have done or what you think is expected of you to do. Even when it is something as simple as a last name change. I don't want any opportunity for you to feel empowered and valued and seen and heard to pass you by. These choices you have will shape you and your spirit, even if it doesn't seem like much of a big deal. There is not a path here that we women must follow, and we shouldn't just give in to doing what others do for the sake of just doing what others have done. Nope. If your mind changes about things because you have spent time thinking about things, and your new way of thinking expands the love for yourself better than before, yeah, go ahead and choose that very thing. It is all about how it improves YOU and YOUR spirit, with every little or large choice you are making right now.

Whatever your thoughts are right now on your last name, and whatever your final decision is, and for whatever reason you chose it, I am proud of you for even taking the time to think about it. You should be too. This is coming from someone who avoided thinking about things for too long back then because it just hurt my entire person to do so. I didn't hear this from anyone—this choice of empowerment with taking my last name back and the freedom it could offer me. I created that significance for myself.

I'm glad you are spending a minute right now to consider what your heart and mind is saying about it. It may feel one way now and be different in the future. That's great. Thinking through things deeply during and after a divorce is self-love, even if you didn't think of it that way. Looking within, even when it's chaotic, is *always* self-love. You are facing difficult feelings all around you. You are facing difficult decisions. But you are loving yourself while you do it. That's big. Take this compliment to heart, no matter how insignificant it may seem. I included this part about a little ol' last name change because it's a choice that can really be something significant in your divorce afterlife if you want it to be. That part is up to you. You can make *anything* a significant part of your personal healing. It doesn't have to be some big, grand thing to have a big, grand meaning to you!

When the paperwork is finished, filed, and final, everything between you two will <u>always and only</u> be about your kids from that point on. Accepting this truth and basing decisions on that is the goal. Bigger picture. Simplicity is key.

You can make *anything* a significant part of your personal healing. It doesn't have to be some big, grand thing to have a big, grand meaning to you!

CHAPTER SIX – NICKEL TOOTHBRUSH

———•❦•———

Here's the hidden gold you didn't know you were getting from me. Welcome to the part in my divorce afterlife that I thought I'd never want to share with a single soul in the whole entire world. But like I said before—when you face something like a divorce, and it's unbelievably more traumatic than you thought it would be, and you make it through the darkest parts—the natural thing you want to do is take notice of other women who might be going through the same thing you did, and promise them they'll make it, too.

There isn't an elegant way to segue into this next part, so I present to you: the breakdown of my breakdown.

I self-admitted into a mental help facility just a few hours after I got home from a lovely Easter Sunday service that my kids and I attended that day. From the time I got home that early afternoon, I could not stop crying in the bathroom. I was someone who was extremely good at hiding personal pain and tears. Not that day. That day, my crying was not easy to try and muffle or hide. I was experiencing a scary kind of hopelessness and was inconsolable. The last time I felt like that was as a young teenager, which led up to an unsuccessful suicide attempt.

That second scary experience on that particular Sunday was roughly two months after my divorce was final and roughly seven months from the date of separation. Yes, *that* much time had already passed, and *that* was the peak of my complete overwhelm with life—over a half of a year later! So, let's forget about any such "timeline" that some believe exists out there for us moms to have made some great and impressive strides in our healing from a divorce. There is NO SUCH THING, and it shouldn't make us feel even more shitty like it somehow does when we're still struggling after six months, a year, or two years! It had been over half of a year when things broke my mind and soul completely! That's where I was, mentally and spiritually, completely broken down. That was darkness.

Going in to get yourself some help when you have a big mental breakdown, self-admitting into a place like that, is just like you think it is. I'm going to tell you more about it because it's very important to me to do so. It takes desperation to get you through the doors of that kind of place. It takes desperation to get you into a car to get to the doors of that kind of place. It starts with the intake process once you walk through those doors. You are first asked if you consider yourself a safety risk (meaning are you wanting to commit suicide), you answer honestly, then you give up every personal item you have on you (just like in rehab and jail), you then get searched to make sure of it. Then, you are given your new Gucci outfit, and the head chef immediately brings your made-to-order dinner right to your private room that includes a balcony overlooking the properties beautiful, lush gardens. Oh... right... sorry... I meant you are given a faded, maroon, scrubs-type looking outfit that feels like cardboard, that is way too big on you, and you also get a toothbrush that looks and feels like it was produced for a nickel. It all *really* pulls the depression and hopelessness together rather nicely. And then you're off! To where, though? Oh, just one of the couches or 35 reclining chairs that are scattered all over this humongous room with the same faded maroon outfits circling around at all hours of the night and day.

So off I went—

to a chair,

and wept...

under a blanket...

with my toothbrush...

for days.

In those days, I don't exactly know what meds I was given, but every six hours or so, I was brought pills with a cup of water. I took them. I was also hit on and ogled at while I was in there. Yes ma'am, that still happens, even when you are in a mental help facility. There is nothing like telling a man to "go away" from you, when there is literally no place to go away to that is out of your line of sight. People smelled. People cussed and yelled random things and made big commotions and every so often got taken out of there by security guards. Showers were interesting... I never felt at ease taking one because it was a bathroom right off the main humongous room everyone was in—so just a single door in between me and the maroon outfit crew. I had one, single, sit-down talk with the house doctor the day after I was admitted, and another meeting with a house counselor the day I checked out. No other meaningful interactions. No hope restored. I wasn't there for the all-inclusive luxury 14 day stay, but I was there long enough to have had enough of the full mental center experience.

What you just read serves as an actual living, breathing, reality that exists in the current world and time that you live in— right here on planet Earth. I am the complete, honest to God, example of how broken a woman can feel after a divorce. And this was seven months after mutual agreement and intention to <u>willingly</u> file for divorce.

Like me, some people in the world will feel so low after a divorce that they'll end up in a mental center, or... they'll never even make it there. That is reality. That was my reality. I believe that even just *knowing* about that scary low that I felt is providing you with the biggest sense of reassurance I could possibly give to you if you've felt this lately, or at all, or right now, in that—you've got what it takes to make it out of any darkness you are in, and I promise you'll be the one helping someone *else* out really soon.

I gained two things from my darkest moment and they have a specific purpose for **you**. The first is:

1. On the day that I was to check out, I absolutely did not want to. I didn't feel like I was actually helped! No one guided me on how to be better or talked with me about anything other than the short convo with the doc. So, I said I wasn't ready to go, and I explained that I had the exact same mindset and hopelessness as when I came in and now I was going to check out and return to the same environment with the same thoughts—how was that helpful? So, a counselor was called over and chatted with me right before I left. We went over breathing techniques to use to steady myself when overwhelm and panic struck me, a safety plan for myself, and he recommended books for me to read that he thought would help. He also set my first appointment in a few days with my very own therapist. That 11th hour chat was enough

to get me to check out, but truth be told, I still would have rather just stayed and slept and took whatever pills they handed me. The therapist appointment was that one lifesaving thing that really needed to happen for me, and that's finally what I got... thank God.

After I started to see a therapist regularly, I felt slightly better knowing I was not actually losing my shit for real. What triggered or caused my complete breakdown was overlooked and untreated depression on top of the expected overall effects of a divorce that were obviously severe enough to catastrophize said untreated depression. Did you know, as with the loss of a loved one, many people also experience moderate depression for the very first time after getting a divorce? I believe that wholeheartedly. A divorce can be extremely traumatizing to beautifully sensitive hearts. And the only ones who will believe that wholeheartedly are the people who've had one.

Be aware not to overlook the possibility that your divorce may be affecting you more than you know. I can't say affecting you "more than normal" because there is no way to gauge that from one person to the next. But be aware of others reassuring you that how you're feeling comes with the territory of getting divorced, especially when you know it's getting to be a bit too much or it's affecting basic daily functions. If you feel that way, please make that first phone call that will get you in to talk with someone within the next few days. It doesn't hurt or hinder a single thing to have a talk with a doctor or therapist for a proper discussion and evaluation when it comes to this. There is a natural, healthy sort of progression through the stages of grieving a separation and divorce, but if hopelessness or a long-lasting feeling of sadness is present, it's time to go talk with someone who can help discuss and differentiate that with you in a professional setting.

You are *so* very important, so therefore it is *so* very important to consider all the ways in which you are taking care of and loving yourself during all of this. And it is important to be honest about the real feelings and thoughts you are having. Now is not the time to sugarcoat shit and prove to yourself you are the capable-at-handling-your-business woman that I already know you are. This stuff is important to be honest about. A professional evaluation and discussion or a checkup and blood draw can also reveal unknown vitamin deficiencies, chemical imbalances that may be literally throwing you off balance, or it can reveal some moderate depression or anxiety or both, based on your thoughts alone. It also serves as an act of self-love with every self check-in and accountability check-in with a doctor regarding your mental wellness and overall well-being.

The intentional breathing technique, the safety plan, and the book recs were all good and well and fine from the house counselor, but I would soon realize that my therapist would be that integral part in managing my mental health.

I could do the things that always provided momentary

relief in my mental chaos over the years, like eating my feelings, or not eating at all for the feeling of having a bit of self-control, or excessive deep cleaning, or sleeping excessively. I could also gravitate toward all the other numbing/avoidant actions that we humans gravitate toward in times of distress—like drug and alcohol use, sex, new relationships, cigarettes, overworking, overspending, masturbation, gambling, or behave in extremely risky ways that are outside of usual behavior. These are a lot of the actions that we choose, because it's self-medicating, it's our quick "self-help" that we control, and it's that instantaneous avoidance from telling people our struggles kind of "help" that makes *those* the easy choices. I've used them all at some point or another in life.

It was no surprise to me that when I voiced my personal need for medication for my mental wellness to a few close girlfriends as we chatted this last year, they too said they were taking medication or had taken medication before to help with their mental wellness during rough times. Like you, I have great, open-topic discussion friendships with my close friends—so how can we not know this about one another sometimes? I know why. It's still not common to talk freely and openly about these things because it automatically makes us feel incapable of self-control and self-care, and then; incompetent because of that. How many people do you know who would enjoy feeling like that? Right—me too—zero. And then to have courage enough to *tell* someone we feel like we're incapable of caring for and controlling our incompetent selves is so far off of the easy self-medicating choices we have within arms-length that we end up not telling anyone. Because we don't want them to think that of us either!

It's uncommon in our human race to announce our mental health struggles, but common in our human race to suffer in silence.

I hope that truth completely flips for humankind.

So, here's how all of this applies directly to you. You're not going to choose any of those easy self-medicating things at any point in your healing. I love you too much to allow it. Fine, I know, I still cannot tell you what you are and are not allowed to do, but I strongly and lovingly suggest you commit to a few sessions with a therapist or counselor.

If you can afford it, wonderful. If you can't, get assistance in your city. It will not cost you anything if you do your research on mental health aide, and please be patient with the initial steps in the setup, as sometimes it takes a while to get a flow going and you may encounter the most rude, off putting people who will make you want to forget even showing up for that first appointment, once you get it. Also, do not be discouraged if it is not a good fit the first session, even after all the work to get it going in the first place. Focus on your commitment to yourself, and be relentless with making this work for you by trying a new therapist, counselor, or doctor. Online therapy has really taken off in the last few years too, obviously, and

I'm certain you can find a therapist or counseling program that fits both your budget and your schedule if you make it your priority.

That concludes my JenTalk; thank you for coming.

I shared my very personal and private experience with you, in much greater detail than I ever would have needed to have your full attention on mental health, because I care about you. I don't want you to forget the importance of the part of your mental health through all this, and I'm pretty sure you won't forget now because of the extra detail. Just like I wanted.

The second thing:

> 2. Out of my experience I was able to see how codependency was very much my way of existing. I realized there, at the mental center, that I was codependent my whole darn life. I didn't even know where or how to begin with changing that... and in staying true to my codependent form, I didn't even know where or how to begin with changing that **without depending on someone else for help**... of course.

Codependency was apparently what I was used to. And let me tell you, some people (me!) will literally not see that truth when they're living it sometimes! After my visit to the 5-star resort and back at home, I didn't see a way out of that codependent existence I was very much used to, being the full-grown woman and mom that I was. It was a part of me, like the freckles on my face, and apparently, how I have existed for as long as I can remember. I was dependent on others to help me with 85% of what I needed to exist. The other 15%, I could manage myself. Not really a good equation there. Are you relating to my equation of codependency at all? A lil bit? A lotta bit?

A divorce quite abruptly shows you what level of codependency you reached within your marriage. Yes, YOU one hundred percent have some codependent characteristics if you were married. I didn't say you were one hundred percent codependent, but I am saying you *do* have some degree of it. This is FACT in every single divorce story, as every single marriage organically develops a level of codependency and interdependency. This is not a yucky word—codependency—it's a very realistic way one can exist, especially in today's world where there are a thousand different ways we are told or shown we're nothing special. Of course, we're becoming more and more dependent on our fellow humans to make us feel significant or guide us in a better direction. We NEED one another in ways we never thought we would or wanted to.

I'd like to have a healthy balance of codependency, interdependency (interdependence), AND independency (independence), to be honest. Pretty sure only one of those is an actual word. But you get me. Look those up. We each travel into and encompass those three ways, one at a time, in different moments and situations our whole life! We all have a bit of codependency. Maybe you already knew that about yourself. Maybe you just read up on what codependency can feel like within relations with people and realize you identify with those needs more than you thought. I am definitely not going to speak any further on codependency as if I'm completely rid of it, because I'm not. But it's a term that I often hated hearing before, but now understand and accept that we've all got some because we are human. So, I'll end this section with the focus back on where I want it to be. Mental health. The benefits that come with the time and effort put directly into your mental health now will stay with you long after this difficult time is behind you.

So, in what specific ways are you going to upgrade taking care of your mental health? Write your commitments down and take immediate action to get something started.

This is mission: critical.

I kept and used that horrible toothbrush for a solid six months after I left that place. I kept it as a reminder that I would never go back there because I was prioritizing my mental health; I would not downplay the traumatic divorce I went through anymore, and I was committed to becoming less and less codependent.

And just like that, with *my* personal experience in the "Fun House," *you* get to keep brushing your teeth with that expensive Sonicare toothbrush you've got!

Congratulations, and you are so welcome.

If you are reading this, this is <u>one single page</u> in a huge life book. Your whole story is still being written!

CHAPTER SEVEN - MONEY MATTERS

---•⚜•---

It's so uncomfortable to talk about—so, let's talk about it.

Did you *both* work and make money during your marriage? Were *you* the sole breadwinner? Did your spouse bring home the bacon? Were you left with $97 and you just happened to be a stay at home mom? Were you both facing bankruptcy? Are you completely loaded and money matters aren't a big matter to you?

Circumstances, circumstances, circumstances.

Facing your money matters and the uncertainty of what it's going to look like down the road, is a tough thing to do post-divorce. I mean, money matters can be a huge stressor regardless of a divorce, but this is the one major thing heading into a divorce that a lot of people avoid looking over right away. However, this must be done at some point. So, it would be wise to get all the scaries out of the whole thing, now.

After this short section, you are going to have a different perspective to consider and will have a solid approach in facing your financials head on. I must say: what an incredible situation you are in if you and your spouse actually discussed the financial situation before or when you chose to divorce, and you had a clear understanding of what that was *realistically* going to look like for the both of you. That was not *my* particular situation, but I have heard of such tales from far away lands. I have learned that many divorcing couples only ever discussed their money matters with such great concern over it during their divorce too! Crazy talk! I was part of that lot.

Exhale and unclench your jaw, relax your scalp, release the tension in your body and the tension you feel over all the money matters as we begin.

In order to move into a new perspective with this, take note of what you are thinking and feeling right now—about money and your current money matters as your mind is now prompted to do so. Financial stability and security *is* a factor in your healing. Financial stability and security can also be a form of emotional security for us. I'm glad you know that and have accepted it. In looking back briefly, be so freakin' real with yourself about the stresses and the reasons for the stresses within the marriage when it came to the money matters, budget, savings, credit, etcetera. Then, again, focus on what YOUR thoughts and beliefs are with it right now—just yours. As you do this pondering, I encourage you to feel thankful and grateful for the financial support and contribution within the marriage, for whomever provided it. You're also allowed to be upset or angered if your financial stability was taken from you and your children without warning, or if there wasn't ever any structure or budget with money at all. If anger does happen to arise, that is an indicator on how much priority you'll have for organization and management with your finances in your future. Right now, allow yourself to feel an array of emotions and have an array of thoughts regarding all the money matters then *and* now.

You won't magically change or improve stuff that you won't allow yourself to truly feel the impact of and fully think through with your own thoughts. You know the drill by now. Acknowledgment of previous experiences allows us to create a new experience with a fresh perspective attached to it.

Surprise! Money completely stresses people the hell out sometimes, both the rich and the poor! I felt all of the emotions and thought all the thoughts regarding the money matters before my marriage, during the marriage, and after the marriage. It ALL stressed me out because I could not unsee what a different financial state I "could have" been in had I just taken care of my own financial stuff completely and separately the entire time. I am totally aware the could/would/should have thinking is unhelpful thinking, but that's what I focused on a few times, and it is definitely what angered me the most looking over my own personal financial standing as a freshly divorced mother of two.

Money matters are another super common source of contention within marriages, duh, and many wonderful people are unfortunately destroyed by it because it was never honestly discussed and looked after on the regular. Some of us were never taught how to manage our money either, so it can definitely be intimidating.

Right now as I am typing, and right now as you are reading, while being completely different times in history, there are couples fighting and arguing over money matters! Those types of arguments will happen until the end of time as well. If that sounds familiar to you, I promise it is okay to laugh about it a little with me just knowing your own marriage wasn't the only one like it when it came to conversing about the almighty dollar.

So, where *I* landed early on at the beginning of the divorce process was, well, not in a good spot all around. Per usual, I relied on my family for everything—financial help being a biggie. Thank God I had them. When I faced my scary money matters, it hit me like a ton of bricks to the face. Whatever money there was that was tied up selling the house was already spoken for with lawyer's fees and all the other things. My family took on all of my monthly payments on everything that had my name attached to it, and that was that. I accepted the money matters as they were and asked myself: at this very moment with money matters as they are, what's best for me, and what would support my ability to raise my children in the best way? The answer was: for me to be closer to my family with all the support, including the financial support. They were in the next state. So, moving a state away, living with family, and just focusing on being a mom was the obvious choice.

Even after the move, just thinking about money or me holding a job and being around happy people with happy marriages, happy situations, happy kids, and happy anything made me panic—then, of course, cry. My depressive mentality was far too low to hold a job. I knew I would likely get fired my first day with my emotional state being like it was. I felt ruined. I felt like the money I had left was what my ex-spouse thought we were worth, remember. I couldn't even provide nourishment or diapers for my youngest on my own. Talk about one of the cruddiest feelings ever as a parent.

How was I going to make money? How was I going to provide for my children? How, why, how, why, how, why... that's all that my mind could spin up. I could not. Stop. Freakin'. Crying.

The ending of the stay-at-home-mom-era...

When it came to me getting a job, like I said before, I winced thinking about how a depressed, divorced, anxiety ridden, (now) chain-smoker mess of a mom would enter any workplace and not just weep the second someone said, "Hi, how are you?" In the second month of my divorce proceedings, my longtime friend suggested I get back into real estate, which I hadn't done seriously in like twelve years. When she mentioned this to me, I was smoking a cigarette, overwhelmed with anxiety, and depressed. So, I cringed, because, like I said, I was in the early stages of hating life. I silently laughed at just the thought of me dressing up and being around people who smiled genuinely at life, while my smile would be real forced and real fake. I remember telling her in that same conversation that I was looking into a local part time cleaning lady position. That is what I felt like I could handle. Scrubbing toilets. I was no real estate broker. Truth be told, I didn't even feel like I would be super great at handling scrubbing toilets either. I mean, I actually like cleaning, and it was pretty much what I thought I had been doing for the last seven years anyhow—cleaning up after people. I thought I could also cry while doing it and no one would know or be around—or really care, for that matter!

As I explained all my sound reasoning to my friend, she stopped me and said in the most loving of ways, "Jennifer, that is far beneath you." I didn't want to hear that, to be honest. I mean, I heard her, but she was wrong. In my mind, I was cleaning lady material. Nothing was wrong with that position, by the way, and nothing was wrong with me thinking that's all I was capable of at the time, scrubbing crap out of toilets. The capabilities I believed I had then matched my confidence. Non-existent.

Despite our conversation, I ended up doing neither the cleaning lady nor the real estate gig. Come to find out, I was only capable of just surviving the day, one day at a time. It wasn't until much later, and with another move to a different city, that I even thought about employment seriously, again. That same girlfriend said she would pay for me to get my real estate license if I said yes right now. I said yes. I studied and finally took the test six months later. Yes, you heard me— it took a really long time for me to get in enough of a stable mentality where I would entertain going out in the world and making my own money. I was not on a linear path. I was all over the place. Still progress. Still healing. Still not embarrassed to say it. When I say really long time, I'm talking a year and half before I agreed to her offer and almost half a year later when I got licensed. A few months after that is when I finally started to work part time and made money for the first time in almost nine years. Some of us are leveled to the ground during a divorce, like I said. Rebuilding from scratch is serious business.

My timeline was completely slow moving with zero "accomplishments" and huge "milestones" and "fast breakthroughs" in the first entire YEAR, as we often like to think will happen. But it was *my* timeline that suited *my* needs in *my* divorce afterlife, and it was the pace I personally needed to survive. That is how long it takes sometimes to get a new and solid foundation set. A REALLY LONG TIME.

However the financial health looked before and during your marriage, it *can* improve and become healthier over time. Believe it. Get that idea in your head. Time and belief and intentional action makes all the things happen. How your credit is right now is one thing to focus on. Now, if you have decent credit and great financial standing currently, this part of the book is obviously not going to do much for you. But, if your credit is no good at this point, there are options to start rebuilding that if that is important to you. Going into your bank, any bank rather, and talking with someone about what they offer for credit rehabilitation is worth doing. Heck, go to several banks and see what programs are available to you with your financial goals in mind. No matter where you are located— I know there is something out there to help kickstart your credit revival should you need it. Now, that is the very rock bottom minimum as far as starting for some, but it is an important beginning that some do not know about. I'm not missing out on sharing any opportunity with you, no matter how small, that supports your forward movement.

You can get a complimentary consultation with a financial advisor; did you know that? Just search around for that; you'll find someone. This will at the very least establish a foundational game plan for your financial organization with goal setting for future financial wellness and stability. Forward movement can look like taking control of your own finances and credit, no matter where you stand after a divorce. It's not easy to look over that stuff at the beginning. I personally did not enjoy seeing where I was at, credit-wise, after the divorce, knowing where I was before marriage. If you're pissed about it—feel that—be in that shitty feeling for a moment. Then, take one small action (mentioned above) that leads you to feeling different about it.

My situation with finances may be like yours right now. If you were a stay-at-home-mom, oh I feel for your every panic-stricken thought. You may or may not have already found employment. You may be relying on your family for everything, like I did. I don't know your specifics, but here's what I do know: no matter what circumstance you are in financially, and whatever fears you have about the future and money... it will all work out.

If there is no family to help financially support you or support you in general right now, there *are* people and organizations out there in your vicinity you should allow to help you in any way that is available. *You* have to be the one to reach out and make it known that you need some help right now. People and help will not come find you. However people offer to help, take them up on it all. No guilt. No shame. None of that. Okay? You'll have to practice that (saying yes to help) if you're not used to it, but you can do it. You are in the accepting mode right now because you know the benefits of accepting things.

Accepting help is no different!

Who are you going to let help you? You need to find these people, and you need to let them help you immediately. You are choosing to be proactive with your methods of stress relief, so here is another way to relieve some stress. If you haven't already, you are going to fill out the forms needed and allow the state to help you with whatever they can offer you. You are going to get food with food stamps if that would be helpful to you. You are going to get help in finding a place to live if you are stressed about where you're going to live. You are going to let the state pay for childcare for your children if that would be helpful to you. You are going to let the state provide insurance for you and your children if that would be helpful. I do not care if your ex-husband is going to keep the insurance on your children, let the state insure your kids as a secondary insurance. Reason being, if and when you get that phone call that your ex-husband can "no longer afford" to insure them, you'll have to do it then anyhow. Accept ALL the help you can get and all the help that is offered to you. That is stress relief that has everything to do with money. You know that is helpful right now!

If you're not *already* going, you are *going* to go to church. "Wait, what? What does this have to do with money matters?" I hear you ask. It is related, and it is not what you think. I am not pushing religion or beliefs on you in any way, shape, or form, but what I am doing is getting you free childcare for an hour or so on Sundays or Wednesdays, or both, while you get a free hot coffee or bottle of water and you just sit down and do absolutely NOTHING but breathe... and sip. Creative stress relief that is absolutely free. Most churches offer free childcare while there is a sermon going on—so take them! Your kids will look forward to it! You do not have to get all fancy. Your kids do not have to get all fancy. In fact, you can just roll outta bed and go. No one cares. I mean, throw a piece of gum in your mouths, but just go. Check them in and go fill up a hot cup of coffee and sit yourself down and just breathe. You don't have to talk to anyone if you don't want to. You don't even have to smile if you don't want to. You don't have to open up a Bible if you don't want to. And you don't have to give up your firstborn to the Sunday evening ritual during a full moon out in the back of the church to show your commitment to their ways if you don't want to. Oh goodness, please know I am kidding—you most definitely have to open up a Bible. Okay, okay, I'll stop that. But you're *going* to go because it is a stress relieving, no cost, win-win situation. So, start looking up where you'll be going this week, right now. Don't wait. Schedule it. Drink all the coffees, take all the breaths, and do NOT do anything except sit and sip.

Let's circle back to food assistance. I don't know everything about it, but what I do know is that the state will most likely give you the largest amount allowed for food a month if you are unemployed or facing a financial hardship due to divorce. Even if you are employed, they may still help assist a bit based on your situation, income, and a few other factors. Accept what is offered.

Do you feel weak or embarrassed at the thought of this, at the thought of receiving any help from the state, or do you cringe at hearing the word welfare? Or state insurance? I sure did at first. It was a huge embarrassment to me. The fact that I had recently been driving around in a 60k Mercedes and had a nearly 4,000 sq ft home filled to the brim with my favorite Costco essentials to now using an EBT food card to nourish me and my children while living with my sister and her family—yeah, that felt like a pretty big reason for my ego to nosedive straight into a pool of embarrassment. In fact, that embarrassment guided some of my actions. I tried to hide it from people when I checked out in the grocery store. From people who didn't care. People who didn't know me, my kids, my ex-spouse, my address, or my situation. But there it was, the shame and embarrassment of being a mother, being depressed enough to remain unemployed, not being able to give my kids the world like every parent wants... and not being able to feed them with my own money. That is what it might sometimes feel like. That is what it felt like to me at first. This is where I am going to provide you with a new perspective, should you want it, and should you be feeling a bit like I did about the whole thing. I sure wish I had this reminder, confidence, and faith in those early stages of the biggest life adjustment I ever had—to know it was not going to be like that forever.

Ready?

You are choosing not to care about the way in which you receive help right now. At all. No matter what help it is and who it is from. You are going to welcome it in so lovingly and be thankful in every possible way for it. That is the perspective to grab onto if it's not the perspective you currently have. You are not living this life for anyone but you and your kids, and you lose no value in who you are as a Mother, Woman or Human right now, no matter how your money matters are and how you are relieving the stress of it until you get it settled and organized.

With intentional practice, you are simply not going to put so much thought into this part if it's that stressful or embarrassing, because you CHOOSE not to. Your *life* is not to impress people. Your life *story* is not to impress people. The ways in which you keep your sanity and how you choose to eliminate any stress is not to impress people. If there ever was a time to adopt the idea of not caring what anyone on the planet thinks about you *or* your life, it is now. You-centric all the way, baby.

I am an amazingly loving, forgiving, sweet, and wonderful person, and it took me a real shitty-of-a-situation divorce to see the freedom in not having to convince another human being of all those things. Your thoughts on your life are what matter here. And if we want them to be good thoughts in regard to accepting help with food, insurance, day care, or whatever it may be, we *make* them good thoughts. You choose them. Thank God these things are available to us in our lives! Thank God they are there to help us right now. This feeling that comes with the help, that we're not good at asking for or receiving; you've got to try to *think* of it in an entirely different way, and you'll *feel* entirely different about it.

Here's my suggestion on what a "different way" to think about it may mean. If you end up deciding food assistance would be helpful, great! I want you to take that food stamp card, whip it out, and use it like it's a Centurion Black card! And while you're using it, I want you to smile like you normally would, be nice to the cashier like you normally would be, have a conversation like you normally would, and just live your damn life. Acknowledge any embarrassment that may come up while you practice this approach. Like when you are checking out in line and there is a nice, married family behind you, and you just know they are going to pay for their sugar free oat milk, raw almonds and organic fruit with cold hard cash. Acknowledge it, laugh at it, and get on with it. You choose how you experience the moment. Acknowledge the embarrassment and break out that no limit bad boy like you're the wealthiest mutha on the planet. Don't forget, I am right there with you when you're there. I was you.

The forward movement with your money matters and your mindset about it all is moving at *your* personal pace; and is not to be compared to any other person's pace. Remember, forward movement is very personal and unique to who we are. It's not a race. There is no same starting point and no finish line.

Your value in the world is never based on anything that is outside of you, especially not your money matters. Your value never changes. It was the same high value when you were married, before you were married, the same high value as it is today, and it remains the same high value in all your years ahead. A divorce, a zero bank balance, bad credit, low self-esteem, and a lot of outside help doesn't change your value, worth, or capabilities.

"I am what time, circumstance, history, have made of me, certainly, but I am also so much more than that. So are we all."

— **James Baldwin**

CHAPTER EIGHT – PARENTING ADVICE

ABSOLUTELY NOT GOING THERE.
YOU ARE DOING AMAZING.
I AM PROUD OF YOU.
YOU'VE GOT THIS.
I SEE YOU.

"All human beings should try to learn before they die what they are running from, and to, and why."

—**James Thurber**

CHAPTER NINE – HEALING

———•❦•———

/ˈhēliNG/ noun: The process of making or becoming sound or healthy again.

At the end of our life, we will all have healed from something, be it a scraped knee as a child to something more traumatic such as the loss of a friend or loved one. And soon you will know what it's like to have healed from a divorce in your lifetime. There is obviously a process to healing, but in every definition I found, there was no mention of a specific amount of time to allow or a specific sequence to follow to guarantee its success. What I *do* know about healing though, is it requires your attention, patience, and maintenance.

Your personal healing will be a combination of so many

things specific to what your individual heart needs. *Your healing will not be like my healing.* Your life story is in your heart, so your healing will naturally consist of what builds *you* up stronger, what gets *you* out of bed, what makes *you* laugh and smile, what makes *you* feel connected to the world and the people in it, and what fills *you* with a sense of purpose and belonging. It's time to run toward those things!

In this last part, we'll stroll together through various things that will support you in your unique-to-you healing process.

Emotional Wounds of Divorce

I know for sure there are emotional wounds you are carrying around right now that no one can see. They are really a thing—emotional wounds—and they are important for you to pay attention to. Emotional wounds can be created by separation, any abuse, betrayal, loss, heartache, neglect, learning a difficult truth about the world, a physical limitation or condition, traumatic events, or performances where unsolicited criticism was forced upon you. When going through a divorce, we can reopen or discover childhood emotional wounds, as they are very much connected to what we are feeling right now. And if you land on the side of extreme thinking and feeling like I generally do, you might have *so many* little emotional wounds that you're unsure of which one needs attention the quickest and the most!

When we intentionally sit in silence, we are better

equipped to hear our emotional wounds tell us how we can care for them. When we listen, those wounds are often translated into the core beliefs we have about ourselves, about others, about our life experience, and about how we desire our life experience to actually be. Uncovering emotional wounds can unfortunately serve as confirmation on how it seems our experiences will *always* be because it's how our experiences have always *been*. It is challenging as an adult to have existing issues to power through in addition to everything the divorce brings with it.

I was often overwhelmed by my existing emotional wounds, overwhelmed to the point of immobilization. Whether that meant unable and unwilling to face reality and get up out of bed or just wanting to go to sleep in the middle of the day to avoid feeling anything at all.

We are absolutely wounded by a divorce. You are. I was. My mother was. My friend(s) were. My neighbor was. My 3rd cousin's ex roommate's dog walker's sister-in-law was, too, after her divorce. A divorce leaves wounds. And these wounds are going to be what you wake up and face every single day. That is, until you wake up one day and just know you are fully healed from them. You'll know when that day is. And you will rejoice in your healing! Or you'll rejoice in your healing from that one single thing that left the biggest mark on your soul. And you'll know when that day is, too! You just will. Your wounds that you are nursing and mending today *will* be fully healed. Do you believe that yet? You will not need a "Fragile, handle with care" label forever.

In a quiet, still moment, with the intention to uncover some wounds, how do you speak to yourself? Plan to focus on this over the next few days. Make a point to listen to yourself. Old emotional wounds show up in our self-talk as beliefs or statements that we are now reaffirming as true in our current hurting. My wounds, in word form, were screaming at me that I had just "dedicated almost eight years of my life trying to build something solid... and for what?" That was on repeat a lot—the "wasted time" wound. That's a common one—the time gone. That thought was always followed up by the wound of "lack of time I had left to start over." There were also previous wounds that were verbalized into the belief that I was *"just a vessel"* for procreation and that I had served my purpose—that was all that was needed, desired, and offered of me, my body. My body that I had issues with now from having children. My follow-up wound to that one was *and for someone who ultimately couldn't have cared less if I woke up in the morning*! Big time emotional wound right there! My childhood wounds were very much intertwined into those. Remember when I said that your emotional wounds from your divorce would tell you your exact beliefs? Yeah, *that* was already an existing wound that was reopened, and it spoke to me in my own voice saying, "Jenn, you're not important or amazing enough, again, to have someone be so grateful that you woke up in the morning." Ouch. That is what an emotional wound is, and it hurts because it is what I personally believed to be true based on similar hurts and experiences in my past. You have yours too, I know. You've already heard your emotional wounds in your own voice, I know. It's just hard to know that's what they are sometimes. Those statements and beliefs that aren't uplifting to you; those are the wounds.

The wounds I was nursing were explicit and angry. That is how deep and loud some of my wounds were, amongst the many others. Those I heard the most. My wounds showed me what healing I personally needed and why, right down to my character and confidence. My divorce revealed to me exactly what my healing was going to consist of, based on my beliefs about my own life story up to that point. I just had to listen.

Listen to your words you're speaking to yourself when you get them. Evaluate them one by one. Whether true or not, *those* are *your* personal beliefs that created the emotional wound. If you really take the time to evaluate, you may discover that some of these hurtful feelings are awful similar to feelings you felt all the way back in your childhood. Truly assess why it hurts so deep. The deeper the hurt means the higher the value you've placed on desiring to experience certain things in life in a better way. Our personal hurts are 100% unmet expectations. This is actually good news! Good news, in that you still don't have to expect others to act in exactly the way you want them to in order for you to enjoy your experiences with them, but rather; you can choose and create how YOU want to experience your moments with others. If you want to heal your emotional wounds, you've got to start telling yourself a better life story.

Self Check-Ins

We're going to have a self-check right now, just like when we were first getting to know one another. If you're not feeling anything pressing for your attention right now, great! Let's still check in and see why you are feeling the neutral way you are so you can continue to do whatever it is to keep you there. Get quiet, hone in on yourself— mind, body, and spirit. Take a few deep breaths and close your eyes and see where your mind goes. Take another minute and feel whatever you're feeling in your body and then come back, and we'll go from there.

Okay, where are you at overall? Neutral, low, or high energy and thoughts? If you can answer that clearly, think of one single way you can raise the overall energy, with either an action or a new thought to meditate on. Is it a glass of water you need, a short walk outside, a shower, a meal, a stretch, reading a positive article, repeating a calming mantra, a phone call to a friend, a 5 minute meditation... *anything* that will invite a refreshed perspective into the moment you're in is the immediate benefit of a self check in. Once you identify what might help, go do that, immediately!

There is and always will be time for a 5-minute self check in, in your day. Always. If you don't think so, go to the bathroom and shut the door for 5 minutes and just do nothing. The world is okay with your 5-minute break from it, and you will see that when you emerge from the bathroom and all is as it was—earth still spinning and air still circulating. You *have* the time for yourself no matter where you are.

It is a good habit to build into your day at certain times or make a point to stop for a quick check in when you feel overwhelmed. Showing yourself love by asking yourself how you are, like you would a friend, is a form of healing. This intentional approach in redirecting your mental and physical presence is invaluable to your overall well-being, too. *You* are in control of you. You're runnin' the show!

Visual Vacation

A different action I want you to consider trying out is intentional self-guided meditation with the purpose of heart rate regulation and steady deep breathing. It is something I myself tried and still try doing in order to "trick myself" out of falling down a rabbit hole of emotional overindulgence. Consider trying this mind trick when you're feeling anxious, which is simply an intentional specific thought involving most of your senses. Yup, again with the "controlling what you can control" jazz—which is yourself! Okay, you're going to create a visual vacation of sorts in your mind. The most calming vacation you can think of. You're not to try to think in terms of winding back time to the "better times" of your life or actual previous vacations, but rather you're going to create a peaceful and content *feeling* and *place* that you can "travel" to right in the moment. Create that in your mind however you need to and make it as personal to you as you can. Try your hardest to get your senses involved. I used good smelling lotion to involve my sense of smell. If you are looking to trick your mind into thinking better thoughts, you've got to go all in sometimes. Yes, even with the nice smelling lotion or a spritz of your favorite scent. Self-love and healing doesn't have to be a complete life overhaul, you know? It can literally be putting on some lotion or perfume and smiling over it for one single little tiny minute of the day as you travel to a peaceful place in your mind. Seriously. Healing doesn't mean paying for a personal trainer to transform your body physically so you can rub it in your ex's face of how great you look, or starting your own business as a single mom to show the world what a "strong woman" you are, for heaven's sake. That is NOT THE POINT and that is NOT THE HEALING you are after. Got sidetracked for good reason and good truth bombs right there. Okay, back to the visual vacation you're going to travel to. In that moment, force yourself to slow your breathing down just a bit and focus for 2 solid minutes on every detail in your peaceful place. Breathe in deep and try to keep in that vision and energy for as long as you can. Really focus in on and see the vivid colors of wherever you're at and listen to the sounds that fit in perfectly with it... inhale the air and all the smells that are there; feel the warm or cold air on your skin; hear the muted conversations of people around you or the waves of the ocean folding into the white sand; feel yourself swaying in a hammock or seeing the sunlight and shadows flicker through trees as you lay on a blanket in the middle of a forest; taste the pina colada and whipped cream or the hazelnut cappuccino as you sip and watch the clouds float across the bright blue sky. That's it; two minutes of intentional focus in a peaceful-to-you place.

You might only make it 12 seconds trying this right now, thinking, "'What the hell am I doing wasting my time creating a fictional place in my mind?" That's okay. Just maybe give it another go when you're not wanting to cuss at me. OR give it a go in the shower, or laying in bed, or the next time you're brushing your teeth for 2 minutes; you know, with that *good* toothbrush. Practice guiding your mind where you want it to go and be intentional on how you want yourself to feel. 2 minutes at a time. This action is reminding yourself that you are in control and are able to self soothe when you need to. This little mind escape/meditation "floated me" until I was past some panic and anxiety over my situation. Often, you just need to break up that thinking loop on purpose and MAKE yourself think about something different. Promise to book yourself a visual vacation soon!

I want you to have various things in your "healing arsenal" that remind you of your mind power and your choices. I mean, you've got to make—force—demand— yourself to do that sometimes; use your mind power. If you have this little trick in your back pocket, it *will* relieve your overwhelm in a small way... just two minutes at a time, two minutes to reset, two minutes, and you may just take your first intentional deep breath for the day. Two minutes for the sake of a calm two minutes that you so deserve.

If this is far from what you're willing to try during this time because it just sounds whack, fine. Everything you are doing to be okay right now is good. It's enough. Everything. There is no one way or one thing that will instantly change things in one sweeping motion. BUT—find one thing that you've never tried before that could potentially help get yourself centered and in a calmer state of mind and try it... at least a few times. Changing up how you've always done things will change up how you'll experience things now.

One Thing at a Time

You can only do "one thing at a time." That's what my sister and therapist repeatedly told me. And now I'm telling you. Don't bend so far that you snap. You cannot do all the things, all the time right now. You cannot change the entire situation in a month. This is adjusting and simplifying your approach. The first time my sister said it to me was when I was chain smoking and I said "look at me—chain smoking—my kids know how much I smoke now, and I'm so mad at myself for it. I need to quit; I don't want them to even see me like this." I was chastising myself for not straightening out my life, beginning with quitting smoking in the first week of my spouse moving out! The absurdity of that!

My sister heard me verbally shaming myself about the smoking and said, "ONE THING AT A TIME, SIS!... you'll get to that, but not right this very second." She was right.

I was going to make it through my days doing one thing at a time and not think I had to quickly fix everything all at once—that included smoking my cigarettes for a little while longer, apparently. So, this is for you to hear as well. Whatever *you* are doing to make it through your day, you are doing enough. Be easy on yourself. You're not expected to be doing supermom things right now. You are not expected to be doing superhuman things right now either. Exhale. And now I want you to inhale and exhale again—deep—and read the words below.

I can only do one thing at a time, and that is enough.

What your healing may look like on some days is saying that one statement to yourself when you feel as though you're not progressing through your divorce like you want to.

Consider all the ways one can heal from a divorce. There are dozens of ways to help you get through each day. And when you feel a bit stuck in your healing, you can try something different.

Write for Your Life

Writing is cathartic. So, of course, I'm going to encourage you to write down all the crazy ass stuff you're thinking about. This is no time to be bashful. Be your whole self and let your human emotions and reactions and thoughts be what they are, without question. Don't hold back a thing. If you really want to experience catharsis, you really must be blunt. If you really want to punch a mofo in the mouth, but don't want to get into trubs, write that out! If you wish you could flick certain people directly into space right now, write that out! If you're so angry and frustrated and full of madness, that you don't even want to share *that* with anyone, write that out! If you're feeling nostalgic and you're overwhelmed with the pain and joy of that, write that out! Write out the details of those cherished memories and your gratitude for having those in your memory bank. It's all a big part of your individual healing—by processing and purifying each thought and emotion that you're having and transferring it to something tangible.

There are no deep dark crazy thoughts that I myself haven't thought of or wrote out. For heaven's sake, us women are such complex feelers and healers that *any* type of heartache or change, or just the experience of motherhood in general, can make us feel completely psychotic at different times in our life! Like, we *really* think we're not normal for thinking some of the things we think and wanting the things we want! And if you don't know what I'm saying with all that, don't worry about it; just skip ahead a bit. But the truth is, women often think in very similar, sometimes whack, ways, whether you believe it or not. You are no lone ranger in any of those often hidden parts of thought that we never admit to. So, I say, write it out! If it looks like chicken scratch on a random napkin, fine. If it sounds like nonsense to your own ears, fine. No one will see it or read it or hear it.

Seriously, no one should see it or read it or hear it! With all your might, refrain from doing this: refrain from writing out and sending off everything and anything you are feeling or thinking to the person or people who are making you feel that sort of way right now, or in a month from now. That action will *not* end up how you think it will or hoped it would. It will not change the circumstances. It will not change the character of your ex-spouse. It will not provide a lightbulb moment for anyone, who then will suddenly give you an apology for something you believe you are owed an apology for. It will not change a thing, because it's meant for only you. Writing things out is for you to express what you are suppressing. That is the purpose of this action. To work through it for you. To release some things from you. No one else.

No one is going to process your thoughts and feelings *for* you, but when they're on paper, in your own writing, you can literally see, touch, and feel a tangible thing that signifies an action you took toward your own healing. That radically affirms to yourself that you do intend to work through what you're experiencing.

If you think it would be beneficial for a friend to check in with you regularly with your writing or journaling and to help you work through what you're experiencing, that's great. The writing part can even be implemented in a sort of open ended back and forth conversation by sharing an online "journal" via Google Docs, or actually writing letters, or even using email. Text messaging obviously works for this too, but if you're not using pen and paper, a separate space that is used only for discussion of your feelings is nice, especially on the harder days when it's hard to reach out but you just want to write 10 paragraphs about what you're feeling. Whatever it is that helps you put words to your feelings and clears out your headspace and heartspace, do that. And repeat, daily. Make it part of your morning ritual, your midday break, or your nighttime routine.

It is also beneficial and important to offset some of that deep and heavy stuff with writing some lighthearted things down. Things that you are hopeful for or words of thanks for something positive you experienced or are looking forward to later in the day or upcoming week. Gratitude entries or acknowledging things you're thankful for is scientifically proven to have a positive effect on your psyche, in that it reduces aggression and enhances empathy.

Voice memo or video logs can reveal and heal a lot too... especially when you know it's for your ears and eyes only. You *can* begin to change what occupies your heart and mind most of the day when you are regularly expressing your emotions through writing. It opens up space for you to fill your mind and heart with more and more positive truths and power statements or scriptures that you find hope and encouragement in. This cathartic cleanse is sometimes only good for the day, the hour, or the minute, but each time you do it, you are practicing self-love. Who knows, your biggest healing might come from writing!

I Just Called... To say...

Have you ever had an unplanned phone chat with a friend on a mundane Monday and it completely charged you up with positive energy that lasted the entire rest of your day and night? I have! And every single time, right before hanging up, we acknowledge how much it has uplifted us both and we say, "You make me feel so great and happy when we talk, thank you." Talking to someone—friend or family or otherwise—for just 10 minutes can brighten your spirit up enough to make it through dinner and homework and a few meltdowns (yours or your child's) before bedtime.

It is true, it works every time. When we're under the weight of our problems, we quickly forget how good it makes us feel when we connect with people we love and care about and who love and care about us. A calm conversation with someone can lower your explosive blood pressure because connecting with someone is an instant stress reducer; it's insane! Connecting with another human being can float you, like a fluffy cloud, right over some heavy feelings and thoughts sometimes.

So, this one also goes into your arsenal of actions to

take for your instant, and <u>legal</u>, pick me up.

Yogee

Google search "15-minute yoga" right now. I know for certain that you could pick any yoga session out of the first one hundred that pop up, and if you did the whole damn thing even completely reluctantly—you'd feel a bit better when you finished. I also know that if you Google search goat yoga right now, you will watch whatever video you were drawn to most by the still pic, then you'll think to yourself, "If someone had a goat yoga session going on right now in my front yard, I would totally do it." Am I right? Of course I am.

What I want you to see with this yoga talk is; one particular thing might not play a really big part in what your healing looks like, like body movement or yoga. Whereas searching up something so random like goat yoga and being intrigued enough by it to want to try it out (because oh my gosh the goats are so darn cute and it's a straight up weird combo I want to do it so bad now) might end up being the biggest part of how you *do* heal just from occupying your mind with new information attached to new, random experiences. Your healing may come from goat yoga! Or from the laughter that happens from looking up funny stuff *like* goat yoga!

Releasing and Letting Go

When we think of the term "just let go of it" or "let it go" we know it implies that we are holding on to something negative that has an effect on us somehow. Working through feelings of offense attached to experiences and people, with the goal of setting them free from your mind and heart, takes time, practice, and creativity.

We tend to include others into our mindspace when we do this because our human experience includes other humans too, of course. So, when you're in your hurt feelings, you often include your biggest "hurters" in your thoughts. When that happens, try this small action to "release" or "let go" of them in that moment. Say to yourself, "This isn't making me feel good, and I might come back to this tonight, but right now; I am releasing all thoughts and feelings." To back up that statement, picture your offender holding a bright red balloon and watch them float further and further away from your sight until they're completely gone.

I was reminded that if there's no "system" or action or prayer or faith behind trying to let go of things, those things will literally not go anywhere! It's as simple as creating something kind of humorous like that to focus on as you give the yucky feelings less and less airtime in your mind. That, and trying out a little thing called forgiveness every so often works well too. Who knows, how you heal might be using red balloons!

Identity

What I know all of us women need after a divorce is to resuscitate our soul and soul identity, apart from being a mom. Whether you think you have your complete and entire authentic identity in this world all figured out or not, I'm certain there are parts of you that had to take a back seat since the moment you became a wife and a mother. That is what you are bringing back to life again.

Big portions of who we are as a whole and how we identify with and connect with others in the world get lost along the way in marriage and motherhood. Our identities are also made up of our interests and hobbies, and those, too, often get placed on the bottom of the shelf in marriage and motherhood. It happens to the very best of us, which is all of us bad ass mothers. And it's okay to not think your identity had been lost *at all* just a moment ago, but realizing right now this very second that maybe, just maybe I'm just a smidge right and some of the things *have* been forgotten that make up the whole of who you are. I really appreciate your open mind with it. That is also what healing can look like for you—considering anything that could evoke more ways for self-love and appreciation.

You know what you are made of, right? In terms of gifts, talents, interests, the things that come natural to you and naturally bring you joy. Think back to before you were married—I mean besides being the wild, amazingly magnetic woman you were and still are. What did you look forward to doing? Walking in the woods? Biking? Painting? Martial arts? Dancing? Drawing? Riding horses? Traveling? Running? Fishing? Singing? Driving around in your car listening to music? Bird watching? Taking cooking classes? Pottery? Knitting? Designing? Hiking? Volunteering? Photography? Getting shitfaced? (kidding, kinda). The list is obviously endless because we all love to do different things, but what's the first thing that comes to mind when I say, "What's an interest of yours that you love doing?"

That's the one. Doing *that* is what unlocking the hidden away you is going to look like. The things you put to the side so you could tend to others; those things are the first things to dust off as you create time for them in your upcoming days. Think about it. Meditate on it like a monk, then write it down! Right now. Three things you enjoy and will *make* time to enjoy within the next 30 days.

1.
2.
3.

Now, pick just one and enjoy doing that one thing within this very week. Make it happen. Make a promise to yourself. Talk about it to a friend or family member and let them hold you accountable in scheduling time to do it, for you. Write it out and put it in your room or on your car dash. Once it is in the forefront of your mind and vision, of what you intend to do, things will begin to show up in how to make more of these things a part of your life and in support of keeping your authentic self authentically inspired.

In the intro, I spoke of the soul work I did after my

divorce. I wanted every single wound I had to be healed, not just the wounds from the divorce itself. The soul work I needed had everything to do with my authentic self and my identity within a marriage and without one. What was it about me and how I experienced relationships in my life that made me forget and question my own identity? Why was I like that? That was the first thing I wanted to get to know about myself. I wanted to thoroughly understand my own backstory! You would think that you know it because it's your own, but just *knowing* it is one thing; trying to introduce new and better feelings into similar experiences or relationships in the present day, and future, takes a whole lot of dedication (and therapy!).

I questioned my overall value deeply after the divorce. I didn't question my value in God's eyes, but I felt so alone in how I viewed relationships, and life, and I even blamed myself for the entire marriage collapse a few times. I wanted to NOT do that anymore. I wanted to be completely accepting of myself in the exact place I was in and with the exact mindset I had, however skewed and troubled it was from the divorce. I wanted self-appreciation and comfort and grace in who I had been and who I was now.

I started searching online about personality types and spent time reading all the various articles, you know, in between crying sessions. Which led me to the Myers-Briggs personality type test (mbtionline.com). I took that quiz, and it was nearly 100% accurate in the breakdown and description of my overall personality and how that "type" experienced life. I read every other one of the 16 types, and none other even came close to it. And wouldn't you know it, my personality type, according to that test, was the 1 out of 16 that was the rarest—with only 2% falling into that personality type. Then it was on to the Riso-Hudson Enneagram personality test. If you're familiar with it, you can probably guess what number I got? Yep, the rarest one again—4. OF COURSE. Lastly, I decided to go deep into Astrology and Zodiac signs and the moon cycles and how the world's energy affects each of our respective zodiac signs. I was definitely matching up to what the signs painted me to be, and all the different readings I came across online were quite accurate, across the board.

Yes, it was a very nontraditional way to "get to know me" a bit more, but it worked in a way that I really didn't expect.

In all that reading and learning I did, I concluded I was not a disasterpiece; I was a masterpiece! I concluded I did not have to change a single damn thing about my complex self, and there wasn't any immediate major improvement that needed to happen in order to love myself right where I was standing.

Reading through all the personality types reminded me of our different perspectives and how differently we each experience life... and relationships... AND heartache. It also reminded me that we **all** question who we are and sometimes purposefully avoid getting to know ourselves because we know we're a little messy.

That led me on the path to the soul work I intended to do while healing. I was going to give myself some well-deserved grace and acceptance. I was going to learn how to better operate alongside others who may never ever think or act or be like me. I was going to relearn how to truly forgive people. I was going to relearn how to prioritize my happiness. I was going to learn how to shut up and listen. I was going to have to relearn to trust and act on my intuition, even when I didn't want to. I was going to learn how to release people that I wanted to trust but didn't. I was going to relearn how to say no and not follow up with any explanation of why I chose that response. I was going to relearn how to encourage myself. I was going to relearn how to be more deliberate in intention and in action and in my words. I was going to learn how to be and express me, again.

My soul work wasn't to adjust my soul or change my identity, it was to reinforce and realign with who I *already was*.

Whichever ways you choose to clarify and reinforce your own identity, take the time to be in awe of your own unique self—the masterpiece that you are.

Focus

When you believe in something so much, you are actually creating the reality of it in your heart and mind, and you really are able to "experience it" somewhat. And whether or not it works out how you envisioned it, the journey of creating it and thinking on it and focusing on it and feeling and experiencing it as though it is actually happening—you will benefit from all the happiness and hope that comes with it.

So, how on earth do I do that, OR, even begin to have a bit of faith and hope in a sad ass time like this? Welp, during this sad ass time, and in all other sad ass times in life, it has everything to do with your mind and nothing to do with your fleeting feelings.

That is probably the hardest concept I have ever had the pleasure to try to understand... and truth be told, I still cannot fully wrap my mind around it sometimes. I am a super deep feeler, and I've based most of my decisions off my fleeting feelings! How is it a mind thing versus a heart-thing? Our heart and soul are our essence, our aura, our spirit; it is US in our entirety... and guess what feeds that? Yep, our mind/thoughts. Then it goes kind of full circle like a wheel that just goes round and round our entire life. Like I said with the fleeting feelings—those suckers come and go. Feelings and emotions can change with a side-eye glare or an unanswered text message! Our feeling of love can shift to disgust with one hurtful sentence spoken or hurtful action taken. It's wild y'all. One feeds the other. But like with the chicken and the egg, what came first? Hard to say, but most of us entertain the same set of thoughts and beliefs our whole life that get locked-in to our system from similar patterns of experiences early on in life, whether happy or sad, and we absolutely SEE and CREATE those same experiences over and over again because it's what we believe *only* exists out there.

I say this because not only is this the time where you are showing yourself a new kind of self-love, you are showing yourself you are capable of believing a new set of thoughts that accompany the new experiences you are creating in your life. This is what your healing may look like.

It has taken me 40 years to scratch the surface on getting my thoughts and my life under my own control. All of that "conditioning" and way of being and thinking comes in loud and clear when we get divorced, and it reverberates off every fleeting feeling like an annoying jingle to an old toothpaste commercial. I remind you of all of that because we so easily get distracted with the myriad of emotions we now feel each day and forget the simple truths of life when we are faced with something like a divorce. All of our core thoughts, especially the negative ones that have been reinforced throughout our life, are the ones that are feeding our heartspace when it aches.

Wouldn't it be a good choice for us to "feed" our minds the positive things intentionally, and not just wait for the world and everything in it to show up like the shitshow we think we're in. Of course that is a good choice to choose! We want to choose the things we'd like to feel or see in the world as we move forward. We want to choose our thoughts as much as we possibly can. Because you know as well as I do, and in staying true to what I just mentioned above, the world and the people and the experiences will ALWAYS show up to us in alignment with our thoughts about those things, separately or as a whole. Our conditioning can really screw us over in our healing if we're not aware of it or diligent in creating some brand-new ways to show up for and love ourselves. That's the *"loving yourself in a new way"* vibe I want you to adopt.

You are the one who chooses what you feed into and really believe in. Grab on to the positive truths below.

- You will see love if you think you will.
- You will feel restored and refreshed if you think you will.
- You will find hope if you think you will.
- You will find amazing, loyal people if you think you will.
- You will have the life that you want if you think you will.
- You will have the love that you desire the most if you think you will.
- You will make money if you think you will.
- You are confident if you think you are.

Now, you are going to actually say the next set of truths below. FOCUS.

- I see love whenever I look for it.
- I feel restored and refreshed right now.
- I feel happiness when I think about it.

- I know some amazing, loyal people, I am one of them!
- I am creating the life that I want.
- The love that I desire the most is available to me.
- I am capable of making the money I desire.
- I am confident right now.

You will see the things you are thinking of the most. So, in this time of reinventing and curating your own new life and mindset just how you want it, the focus needs to be clear. Your thoughts need to have your real hope attached to them. Think up and dream up exactly what it is you want to see and feel. Choose the thoughts and practice every chance you get.

Don't Stop Believin'

Have that child-like faith that it will all work out for you beautifully! Do not disregard how important certain things are to you in life. Do not get rid of your idea of the beautiful life you want. Nope. Hold on to it. That's important to you, and there is still every reason to believe that you will have it just the way you want it in your lifetime! You get to create another one right now. Another lifetime!

Your imagination and intentions are opening up, and your mind is entertaining thoughts of hope. If it is loyalty and faithfulness that was broken but that is what you desire most, and the narrative you are telling yourself now is that no one can ever be loyal and faithful, you go wash your mouth out with soap, young lady! Because guess what? People are loyal! YOU WERE! People can be faithful! YOU WERE! And YOU are someone, aren't you? Of course you are, and you're an awesome someone! So that means there are loyal and faithful, awesome people who exist in this world! You're one of them! So am I! Boom. Don't stop believin' that there are millions of people in the world who are also loyal and faithful and want the same thing as you!

If a long-lasting marriage is what your heart still desires, you can have that. You don't have to think about that right now or think about getting it right this very second, or even in 5 months, but your deep desires for happiness alone are confirmation that those things DO exist in the world... or you wouldn't be able to feel that desire so deeply in the first place!

Healing is taking yourself and your dreams into consideration a whole heck of a lot more than you have been. I'm making sure that right now, today; you remember you are a living and breathing woman who is complete. Complete and whole. Nothing is missing from you. And while your children live in your heart and soul for eternity, they remain living and breathing people, outside of you, too. They are complete and whole, just like you.

You can be the most loving and caring and giving woman, mother, friend, daughter, and sister and also be unapologetically dedicated to keeping yourself happy first, did you know that? Isn't that some insane truth? Like, what selfish wench does that? Be happy… *FIRST???* Seriously though, did you know that you can and should do that? I didn't. Until after I was divorced! You can do that, be happy first! You can do that in your apartment. You can do that in a 10,000 sq ft home. You can do that in a mobile home or in a motel or on a scooter or riding a Ferris wheel. You can be happy FIRST without all the explanations! Incredible!

The feelings of hope and happiness and contentment and peace won't just show up for you in your hurting, but it is very much available to you at all times. Some of the smallest of actions out there for you to do for yourself can invite in the biggest moments of hope. Alone time can be just as healing as being around those who fully support you and love you. Solitude allows for you to rest or read or pray or just sit in silence and hear your own breath. A hot, bubbly bath every night for a week can be healing to both your body and mind! Meditation can be just as healing and comforting to the mind and soul as opening your Bible and meditating on the Word can. And, by the way, you can be a believer, an atheist, or anywhere in between to do either or both those things, meditate and open up a bible. Doing things differently, or reading different things, or trying to think differently about something through repetition and practice is self-love in action. Stagnant minds can create real crappy scenarios. Change it up. You're on a new path. Movement changes your energy on purpose, both body movement and mind movement. If you're laying in bed and spinning up in sadness, try with all the strength and power you have, and get up and go outside and get a few deep breaths of fresh air in your lungs. These little things are choices that are loving toward yourself. Going for a walk is just as healing as reading up on or listening to something inspirational or encouraging. Talking to a therapist is just as healing as journaling about your thoughts. PICK ONE. TRY ONE. TRY SOMETHING. ANYTHING.

Making time for things that will allow moments of hope and happiness to take over is so important. Laugh at everything you possibly can for an entire day. Just look for something that makes you laugh or smile. Look for it, you'll find it. Try yoga or meditation or praying for the first time. Pick one thing and do it every day for 10 days. 5 days. Tomorrow. Right now.

"Something that you are *choosing* to do is always going to feel better than letting whatever yucky feeling come in and take over."

Go harder if you want, go 30 days of something "new" to you. You are not going to heal to 100% with doing one new thing in one single week, but a solid month of choosing to think one happy thought the moment you wake up or doing a seven-minute breathing exercise or taking a shower a 5 am and getting dressed with full makeup and hair done or praying for 50 seconds or writing down one thing you are grateful for, *will* do something positive for your mind and heart.

You want to know another way you're going to heal from all this while practicing that pure self-love? You're going to give yourself complete grace right now for not wanting to do any of that stupid ass meditation garbage or breathing in that bullshit outside fresh air that I suggested! Give yourself a break. You have your healing and self-love repertoire fully stocked and ready to go. As time moves along, you *will* organically, with all your wonderful might and for the sake of your own well-being and sanity, find something new to do that adds to your overall good health and well-being. You will do it, and it will feel amazing, and that will be that.

How You Heal

You choose how you want to move forward starting today. You have lots of choices ahead on how you heal. It is *all* your choice and there is never a "wrong" one.

How you might heal is you rely on everyone around you for every single thing when you're in your darkest moments and when you feel hopeless. How you might heal is you chain smoke cigarettes, and you chug coffee for a bit. How you might heal is you cry yourself to sleep, feeling like a worthless pile of trash as you're lying next to your soundfully sleeping children. How you might heal is you forgive your ex for anything and everything that you feel was not right or unfair to you or your kids, and then forgive your ex again the next day when you feel upset about it all over again! How you heal is you vow to never talk trash about your ex in front of your children ever, and you choose that each day for eternity. And I mean that with every serious bone in my body wrapped in all my beliefs and convictions. How you heal is you accept that you will love and be loved again. How you heal is realizing you are not a puppet-master and cannot control one single person on the face of this planet, so learn to release all strings and watch things that offend you float away on little red balloons. How you might heal is you make jokes and laugh about every single funny thing you encounter from now until forever. How you might heal is you write about your life story as you're living it. How you heal is by loving every inch of your own body in the condition it's in right this very second, and you do that each waking day from now on. How you heal might be goat yoga. How you heal might be seeking out other divorced women so you feel seen and supported in every way. How you heal might be trying meditation for the first time and you think this freakin' meditation crap isn't going to do anything… but… then… it… does… and you never look back and you start to crave the moment where you can say, "Yep, time to go calm ALL the way down and meditate." How you heal is you pray. How you heal is you don't care people might not like that you've just asked them to pray. How you heal is you let friends fall on whichever "side" they fall on after your divorce, and you love those around you **even harder** than before because they're still there. How you heal is you inhale deeply right now and exhale deeply right now… and you realize, "Holy moly, breathwork feels so good, and I really *can* shift my own energy on purpose with just slower, intentional deep breathing!"

The way in which you heal might be 150 different ways that change over the next 150 days. Healing doesn't mean one way or another way. Healing doesn't mean <u>action must have intentional action every single minute of every single day or I'm falling off the healing train</u>. No, no, no, no. Healing is making it through your tough days. Healing is making it through your not so tough days—whatever that may look like. What matters most is that in each and every one of your days, you are aware of your innate value, and do your best in making choices that support that awareness!

The truths that I'm going to share next, you may not see, but they are surrounding you right now. They're there, and you'll be able to see it all clearly in your future when you look back at this time.

-You are loved so much by either yourself or someone else that this book, with my words, was gifted to you so you would be reminded of that love.

-You *already* knew your worth because you invested your time into yourself by taking action and reading an entire book.

-Even the action of taking in a deep breath or two over the previous chapters, like I asked you to, is action that confirms you knowing your value and having a strong mindset for self-love.

-You've listened to some of my suggestions with an open perspective, and you cared enough about yourself to kindly consider these positive actions in order to move forward in your life.

-You, my smart and irreplaceable woman, already made up your mind that you are absolutely going to heal from this because you opened this book.

- Hope and strong faith for your new, amazing life was already in you, and now that hope and strong faith is fortified just by you moving your mind through perspectives other than your own.

My intention was to meet you *somewhere* in your divorce timeline; share some open women-code with you and address some things you might try to hide to remain on the "pretty" and "under control" and "got my life together" side of divorce things. I, myself, never responded well to those articles, books, or that kind of advice when it was me hurting alone at the beginning. I didn't *want* to hide things; I wanted to heal every wounded piece of me. All of it.

Understanding and acknowledging real hurting and real healing was what I was after. There are those who will never think or understand how much a divorce can actually impact your soul. But it is very much a grieving process, in that you are grieving the loss of a shared life and responsibility with someone who is still very much alive and will *remain* a part of your life for the rest of your life because of your children.

No divorce, circumstance, or any other person can tell you what and how your life is going to be now. You're not just going to trickle off into the night and go live an uninspired, mediocre life. No freakin' way. You chose to be Y O U again! That means you get to experience your divorce afterlife however you want. Think incredibly happy! Think fully healed! Think bold! Think confident as hell!

In your divorce afterlife, you may experience sunsets and moonrises like you've never experienced them before! You may write that book you've always wanted to write! Or finally say yes to yourself and become your own boss! You may feel gratitude in a way you've never felt before! You may perfect a skill that you dabbled in as a child! You may feel good in your own skin for the first time in your life! You may creatively express emotions you've been keeping inside for a long time! You may help another mother out in her darkest hour! You may see the world in brighter colors! You may deepen your friendships! You may discover something totally rad about yourself that you didn't realize existed! You may finally take that dream vacation... alone! You may even exchange friendly *Love Yous* with a movie star in your divorce afterlife!

You just <u>never</u> know how amazing your human experience can feel and be until you start dreaming it up... *exactly* how you want it. Then, making one single, intentional, self-loving choice at a time that supports the genuine you and that genuine desire; all while taking just one breath at a time.

That is how you heal.

And *that* is how your **DIVORCE AFTERLIFE** becomes simply…

your **l i f e**.

NOT THE END

BONUS CHAPTER – LOVE AND RELATIONSHIPS

A s of writing this today, I have been married once; I have been divorced once. And I am certain I have never received or given love the way the deepest part of my heart and soul desires to most. Am I sad about it? No. Yes. Some days it's no and some days it's yes. If you haven't experienced the love you desire the most either, you know how back and forth that longing for it can swing. I am hopeful for the both of us that we will experience love so profoundly in our new lifetime, that we will be certain it's the love we've been expectant of our whole life.

We each know in our heart of hearts what we "think"

love is supposed to feel like and look like, despite how we were raised with or without it. We know how affection and adoration was displayed around or near us or to us, or how it was "taught" to us or not. We have our own understanding and example of what love is and means to us individually. We all know that love cannot be explained, and love cannot be bought. We all know that unconditional love isn't truly felt or experienced by everyone. We know we all desire love, in some form. We know that love exists, still. Right? Of course we do.

There is no need to question why you might feel absolutely disgusted thinking about future love while reading these words right now. I wasn't even thinking about that stuff at all when I was freshly divorced. It wasn't until YEARS later that I thought about it and actually got happy and excited about the idea! **Here's your warning now:** come back to this later if you don't want to think about or are not ready to think about love and relationships right now.

So, what is it going to feel like when you're ready to meet someone new and start going out with romantic partners? What's it going to be like when love starts to grow in your heart for another person? **It is going to feel and be amazing, of course**—especially because you didn't shut your heart up, even while you were mending it!

I penned this out (below) when I started to realize I was ready to meet and get to know some new people. This is the reality of what it may feel or be like for you when you're ready, too.

1000% NEW

At 38, there are still feelings and thoughts I haven't experienced yet. I haven't really considered that... until now. I guess I just thought I'd take the same emotions I've always had and would feel and think the same way about certain things in life, despite getting older, because I have 38 years of "training." I thought if I was good at meeting new people in my 20s, how hard could it be in my late 30s? I mean, I do have way better jokes now; I have genuine interest in people other than myself, and I'm sober. I thought once I was over the sting of divorce and ready to date, I'd have a date... that night. I never really thought about THIS being a "new" experience—dating. I thought it would be like riding a freakin' bike. You find, you meet, you like, you date. Easy peasy. Yeah, nope. This is something that has little familiarity and little comfortability. And while, yes, we are smart people, and yes, we can figure how to work through things, and yes, our thought life evolves with age, and yes, we tend to have more discernment with decision making on super important matters, especially after becoming a parent; that's not what I'm talking about here. What I'm talking about is—we have never felt the feelings and thought the thoughts that inevitably come with trying to put yourself out there in the dating world after a divorce.

This is 1000% new.

This takes up our precious time and a decent effort to find someone to invite into our life, because we're looking to find someone of real value versus someone for just the night. And this time consuming, advantageous feat commences—all while trying to still get settled into our new "normal" being a single parent, which actually exhausts the dating scene motivation right out of us if we're honest. Until we get lonely again when all kids are quiet and self-entertained—and, well, we are alone. Then we get motivated in the moment to connect with someone/anyone just to avoid feeling alone for long.

We are going to try to juggle this while putting some of our needs and desires first to keep our sanity, without feeling like a monster of a person for making our happiness a big priority. I mean, we are dealing with lots of things as solo parents, but our happiness does set the tone of our new, everyday family dynamic with our children. We should totally prioritize it because we ALL benefit from a happy parent. When it comes down to us solo parenting now, in hopes of duo parenting again someday, it is <u>new</u> feelings and <u>new</u> thoughts. Solo parenting in itself is ALL NEW—ALL THE TIME. But this life chapter is a whole other level of our human experience.

See, after you hit that point where you are ready to consider sharing your time with someone on some dates, or just are excited to flirt with the opposite sex, it's going to feel like you really suck at it once you start. Once you have your dating vision in place when you go out in public, you'll probably start playing the LET'S LOOK FOR WEDDING RINGS game with yourself, and you will definitely be disappointed by the amount of times you'll lose playing this game. Because EVERYONE is taken, and you are literally the only single person on the planet. Or that's how it will seem, at least. You might occasionally stare at random couples at the grocery store and think "THEY can find someone, but I'm single?" as you roll your eyes then look down to check yourself out and size yourself up to a solid six while sighing a little bit thinking about your bangin' body... before kids.

You'll probably even have some regrettable conversations that lead to absolutely zero fulfillment of any kind... at all... whatsoever. You are probably going to spend time filling out your attribute-sales-pitch biography on every dating app ever created, hoping either your impressive face/body, your impressive title, or your impressive words about your overall awesomeness, snags you a date. Then, when you finally realize, after a while of receiving horrifyingly boring messages about how your day is and what you are wearing, that it doesn't really matter what you say in it. It then becomes another entertainment platform that sucks up time and you're then going to start writing things in there like "can eat a whole pizza alone" and "impressive words impressive words" and "not sleeping with you"... and roughly get the same amount of matches and interest. Because a lot of lonely people are fast, easy, and cheap, and a lot of people just play that numbers game with dating these days. That sad fact will leave you feeling the feelings and thinking the thoughts that this just can't be "it" with dating. But alas, it is actually just the beginning stages of this new experience. Hooray! It gets better though... I think.

You may have conversations with genuinely interesting people, but not your type of interesting. And that's alright. That's a healthy part of normal life, dating radar aside. You may also actually make more eye contact and smile at people in real time, and it will feel so good. You might even go on a date and laugh and have fun and enjoy the moment for exactly what it is—a moment—with someone you thought had an attractive enough face to not mind staring at it for an hour in real life. Point is, it is being open and ready and accepting of the new thoughts and the accompanying new feelings, too. So think them and feel them. And say yes to people.

I don't know it all. I especially don't know how to balance trying to get out in this dating scene and be a Grade A parent, a good family member, a good friend, and a good breadwinner. I have never done it. Have you? If you have, write a book and sell it to me. I will literally throw my debit card at you. Honestly though, we are all such different people; we cannot take any real advice we hear on it to heart. But my hope for us all is that we can find humor in it and still press on with optimism in our new life. No one really wants to be alone, so laugh knowing you are in good company, and be encouraged that we won't be alone forever.

Balancing this new time we want to spend with our heart kind of exposed to fast rejection is a crazy big challenge too! Not only are we trying to keep our good spirit afloat while having the mark of divorce in our life— well, life is probably not how we pictured it to be at the moment, no matter how grateful we are to just to be alive every day—the rejection will happen, unless you find your unicorn on the first go. Which, btw, piss off. If rejection does happen though, do not grieve the loss of someone who was clearly not God's pick for you! Keep moving, because what is ahead is something special.

It is an ongoing adjustment to life after divorce. It is super scary exciting scary exciting (in that order, and repeat). But I do know it is a very welcomed mix of feelings from the other feelings that only a divorce can bring out. A brand-new experience still, and not as easy as we hoped it would be to navigate. Keep a light heart about it if you can. It will all work out.

It is so funny the things we tell ourselves sometimes to cheerlead our fears and doubts right on through the unknown of a new, solo life. It's as if once we're ready to get out there, we expect quality people to connect with— to come easily to us, and not in the biblical sense. We expect people our age will have not already totally given up on wanting to feel some extreme form of love interest again, not just in the biblical sense. We expect to weed out the obvious "not what I'm looking for" with some basic deal breaker Q&A and expect to mutually go all in with the one who genuinely invests a little bit of their time into having some of our time. We expect these things when it is what we, ourselves, desire. But it seems to be a full-time job, this "dating after divorce gig." We get lazy (because parenting is work, yo) and we lower our expectations, and then we get lower quality interactions. We then are feeling like we have our crap together this week and we heighten our expectations upward. Which ends up writing off more than half of the free world because we are all imperfect, broken, filthy sinners with imperfect, broken, filthy pasts... and kids. Last part of this is the expectation adjustment to a complete zero. When we are lonely, our expectations then are adjusted to what our flesh wants, instantly. That is a risky one altogether. Not recommended. Go for a run.

There is also a big expectation we have of ourselves in this new gig: we expect that we will keep our feelings about this new experience in check.

But we won't.

We're going to start feeling some sort of way when we're intrigued by someone. And in some sort of way, it's going to tell us about our actual emotional availability. We should definitely listen to it. If it feels scary, good, but you're cautious and scared, but it feels good... don't let the scary future thinking destroy the good feeling you have about it today. Don't freak out, you big freak.

Here's why. We have not had this new experience with these new people we meet before. Ever. We have no clue what this could possibly feel or look like in the future. We shouldn't limit the potential of these new interactions based off of our most recent, significant love history. I believe that the only way you can truly "check" your emotions with someone else is if you're back with the same person you've already loved before! There is learned history with old love and there obviously was a checkpoint and then a limit between you and the ex.

Don't forget that this, however, is 1000% new.

The closest emotion-filled experience our mind, heart, and body has felt prior to this new one was the experience tied to our divorce. And who can say that experiencing a divorce didn't suck? No matter what the circumstances were. No one. Divorces suck. So, basically, we are literally trying to force our mind, heart, and body from protecting us (what it is made to do) when we start to open up the ideas of trying again with someone new! Our minds are like NOOOO!!! DANGER! YOU FREAKIN' IDIOT! Did you not just feel that back there? Why are we going here AGAIN? STOP! TURN BACK! That's when people often start prepping the brick and mortar, and up go the walls. But it is such a disservice to ourselves and our true nature to deny all the good feelings God gave us as a way for us to "protect ourselves" from the bad feelings we have felt and didn't enjoy.

When we block one feeling off, they unfortunately all go away. Same with avoiding feeling some sort of way; you won't feel much at all. That's boring.

We cannot let those more recent sucky feelings diffuse the new fiery ones that come with this new experience. Those fiery ones are the motivators! And there is nothing like it. We should always chase those feelings and the people who sparked them, because so few people in life can bring those out (do not mistake the fiery bedroom feelings with what I'm saying either, because those ones are actually subpar in comparison to the real deal if you're not truly invested in them). See, we expect to keep and control our feelings in a realistic manner when we get out there, but if we're wanting someone to see us and our whole heart and like it and vice versa, we're all in, and that really means ALL of who we are is in it. There's not a switch where we can just determine the amount of emotion we start feeling in our new experience. We're going to feel some things that we may not know what to do with. Know it. Expect it. Enjoy it. Our whole heart, our love and our happiness has no cap. Yes, courtship has value, but feeling something and enjoying good feelings has value, too.

The following is a very real and very human thing for us to do in the beginning stages of being ready, willing, and able to start dating. We will continue to question our date-ability if we don't find an interested party within one minute of announcing to the single community I'm here.

How we question our date-ability is by questioning everything about ourselves, duh. We'll question our age, our body, our face, our bad habits, our schedule, our talents and skills, our family dynamic, our beliefs, our sins, our secrets, our parenting, our patience, our hygiene, our work ethic, our hairline, our humor, our past, our future, our dreams, our desires, our overall value, and our bank account balance—and we're definitely going to question WHO is really worth us questioning ourselves about, anyhow.

The post-divorce-collateral-damage-self-assessment is coming no matter what.

*But good news is: you're awesome, and you'll survive it. Welcome it in like a lost puppy and be kind to it. Just promise me that while you are assessing the "damage," you are also staying so very much in love with some of the best things that make you, **you**. You're all good from the ground up, love, and you are **<u>totally</u>** dateable.*

This is what humans do best though, right? We self-assess, not only to keep us happy with being exactly who we truly are, but to also assist us in recalibrating anything that will support our ongoing happiness with ourselves while we are in search of someone to give a darn about again. You get to choose who you want to entertain or allow in your world, you're not waiting to be "chosen!"

Last thing. Another fun element to this new experience is—the element of surprise.

You'll be surprised at your willingness to actually try to gauge someone's intentions with your super senses quickly, and still be nice about not really liking what you're picking up on them. You will also be surprised by your ability to **just stop talking to someone.** *It is a part of entering this world of dating. It's not a super fun part, but it is necessary. It doesn't feel right, but again, sometimes totally necessary. Especially when someone talked to you for four minutes and is buying a plane ticket to come see you. Just... stop... talking.*

You will probably not be surprised with the people who will absolutely say whatever it is they think you want to hear to get into your head and your bed. The surprise factor does have an upside though. You will be surprised at the amount of single people there are out there, that are all probably a bit lonely like you when the sun sets, and that even by just trying to connect with them (however new and impersonal it feels at first) you are that much closer to your heart experiencing love in a whole new way.

Wanting THAT very thing should not be an element of surprise to us though. We were made for this kind of stuff. And I truly believe we will all find it if we're open to it!

You are 1000% renewed, enough, and you are loved,

Jenn

What's it going to be like when you wake up and immediately smile because it is a brand-new day, and you have fun plans for the day with friends or your kids or the love of your life? **It will be and feel amazing, of course.** And if that's what you want, it will happen by you getting up tomorrow, and the day after that, and the day after that.

You will not be in the same space, have the same mentality, or be the same woman in one year's time. It will look and feel different. Be better. Solid. And there will be a major sense of personal growth, accomplishment, peace, and freedom.

You will move on from this time in your life with a heart full of love that you'll be excited to give to someone, and I can't wait to hear about it!

"Healing doesn't mean the damage never existed. It means the damage no longer controls your life."

— **Akshay Dubey**

AUTHOR BIO

Jenn Logan is a mom, real estate agent, writer, and debut author from Ruston, Louisiana. She currently resides in Oregon with her family. A mental health and happiness advocate, she was inspired to share her experiences after divorce and the realization that many women were suffering through it as she was. Using humor and an open and honest narrative, she shares tales of surviving a divorce, prioritizing mental health, and all the real thoughts of a newly single mom. Logan has always loved words, from becoming the first Entertainment Editor for her high school newspaper, a life-long journaler, and occasional blogger, avid reader, and now an author, she recognizes and appreciates the power words can hold. When she's not writing, she loves to drink iced coffee, sing, laugh with friends, dig her toes into a sandy beach, and gaze into the night sky. She's vocal about the comfort and strength she receives through her therapy sessions and how fabulous her "happy lamp" is. Her kiddos bring the most genuine love and joy to her life daily, and Logan helps spread it around by smiling and laughing persistently, even if it is not always easy.

Her second manuscript *Prozac and Macchiatos* is set for a 2021 release, and her third is underway.

www.jennlogan.me

Hello reader,

If my words have been helpful to you in some way, please consider leaving an honest review on Amazon so other mothers can find the book easily if they're searching for it!

Love and hugs,

Jenn

Made in the USA
Las Vegas, NV
21 December 2021